Growing Great Characters From the Ground Up

A Thorough Primer for Writers of Fiction and Nonfiction

by Martha Engber

Published by Central Avenue Press
Albuquerque, New Mexico

Requests to make copies of any part of the work should be
mailed to the following address:
Central Ave. Press 2132-A Central SE #144 Albuquerque, NM
87106

ISBN 10: 0-9715344-8-9
ISBN 13: 978-0-9715344-8-3

Library of Congress Cataloging-in-Publication Data

Engber, Martha.
  Growing great characters from the ground up : a thorough primer for
writers of fiction and nonfiction / by Martha Engber.
      p. cm.
  Includes bibliographical references.
  ISBN 0-9715344-8-9 (pbk.)
1. Characters and characteristics in literature. 2. Fiction--Technique. I. Title.

  PN218.E54 2006
  808.3'97--dc22

                                        2006026821

Cover photography by Kyle Zimmerman
Book design by Dugan Holt

Central Ave. Press
2132-A Central SE #144, Albuquerque, NM 87106
www.centralavepress.com

Printed in the United States of America

Table of Contents

Introduction

Believable characters are the most important feature of any book, whether fiction or nonfiction, because even if you're a genius at telling a story, readers won't follow for long if they find the people you're writing about dull, one-dimensional or unbelievable. While you might already know this, you probably also know that creating and developing great characters are tasks easier said than done.

Why You Should Buy This Book

I'll show you that creating truly great characters does not begin by staring at a blank page or computer screen. Rather, the process is completely organic and begins inside of you. Instead of encouraging you to get in touch with some mysterious inner green thumb, however, I'll delve into the concrete skills you'll need to seed, grow and ultimately shape your characters.

Along the way, we'll take a look at a variety of examples from past and present literature to further illustrate the process. I'll also provide exercises at the end of each chapter, which if completed, will help you create and develop your own characters, so after finishing this book, you'll be able to put it down and let the characters lead onward. While a marvelous prospect, an even better one is that as your characters grow, you will, too. Not only will you develop an ability to think at an almost microscopic level, but you'll come to appreciate that it's only by getting your hands dirty and working hard that you can achieve what you most want, characters who don't just grow into average specimens, but rather bloom into gorgeous, unique and eminently believable beings.

Part I: The Groundwork

I didn't learn to garden organically all at once. Rather, I learned my way into it. I discovered that it takes a special way of thinking about the soil and the life in it, the things that grow in it, those who garden and eat from it, and the nature of which it's a part.... You will find that this way of thinking affects more than your gardening. It can come to color the way you look at life in general.

— *Your Organic Garden With Jeff Cox*, by the editors of Rodale Garden Books

Chapter 1
What's a Character?

The old chicken and egg joke could well be rewritten for writers as follows: *Which came first, the character or the plot?* The answer is that it doesn't really matter. What does matter is understanding that stories must revolve around people. That's because we humans never tire of trying to figure out who we are in relation to each other and our surroundings. So if you have a basic concept in mind — for a novel, short story, creative nonfiction book, biography, play, etc. — this book will help you determine who will populate your story. If you're beginning with a certain character in mind, this book will help you develop the character and in turn, the story, by getting you to focus on what problems the character will have to surmount.

If you already have both a character and basic plot in mind, you might be tempted to start writing and let the tale grow as it will. While some famous writers dig in as such, most of us would hit rock almost immediately, having no idea yet as to who we're writing about or why. So instead, let your story incubate for a while as you read on. Not only will you give your story the time it needs to gradually expand, but the time you'll need to plan for the actual writing. After all, creating and developing characters is remarkably similar to planting a garden, in that success depends on how well you prepare, and the more thorough the groundwork, the fewer the errors and the more spectacular the outcome. You'll end up with terrific characters while cutting your rewrite time in half.

Now that we're ready to begin, what better question to ask than, *What is a character, anyway?*

Generally Speaking

The word *character* has a multitude of definitions. Brushing aside its uses relating to secret codes and genetics, the word can also mean *a combination of qualities, a distinguishing feature, possessing moral or ethical strength* and *acting in a certain capacity*. While intriguing, none of these definitions helps us understand the word in the context of writing. Not until, that is, we reach definition number eight or so — *a personage* — which is exactly what we're looking for. A character for our purpose, then, is a person, and a person is a living, thinking, feeling human being.

Our task is now a thousand-fold more clear: to create and develop characters who actually *live*, even if only in our imagination, in the memories of others or in the documents of history. While this may seem obvious, think of how often you've read a book in which the characters were no more than tools for fulfilling the plot, mere things to be sidelined when the fast action, cool technology and complicated plot twists begin. Or think about books you've read where the author was so bound to dates, places and other historical facts that the characters turned into dry museum relics. Do we really care for these characters? Maybe, but only until we reach our destination — the mystery solved, the crises passed — after which they're forgotten.

But do we ditch people we truly love? No way. If we have a deep appreciation for their complexity and worth, we'll make sure they stay front and center at all times. Does that attitude reflect loyalty? Yes. Does loyalty lead people to stick around until the end? You bet. Is that how we want our readers to feel about our characters? Absolutely!

To make that happen, we have to go beyond simply designing characters to actually breathing our life and energy into them. When we do so, we'll shift from writing stories populated with people to understanding that people *are* the story.

As Pertains to Fiction

Fictional characters are people born from imagination. While this might seem an oxymoron — because how can characters be real if they're made up — it's not. If we're real, then what we create is real, too. Consider an artist who creates a piece of sculpture or a master gardener a fabulous public garden. Although the sculpture and garden are products of the imagination, they nonetheless exist for all to see and experience. The same is true for the characters we create. Since our characters also will be publicly displayed, we should devote as much time, energy and attention to detail in creating them as the sculptor and gardener. If we take this responsibility seriously, so will our readers.

As Pertains to Nonfiction

Nonfiction characters are people born in real life and filtered through the imagination. While everyone understands the first part, not all writers understand the second.

One of the reasons writing nonfiction is so attractive is that the story comes with readymade characters. Unfortunately, some authors erroneously assume there's no need for character development.

Many writers undertake nonfiction because they enjoy research. That preference is usually accompanied by a strong desire to present an unbiased view. Though laudable, it's also impossible since there is no such thing as an unbiased view. Though born in reality, nonfiction is filtered through your brain, your imagination, and your experience. If you deny that by cutting yourself out of the picture — your impressions of and connections to your characters — you'll also cut the life out of them, reducing them to boring one-dimensional figures.

It's far better to admit that you're telling your characters' stories through your own eyes, and then get down to the business of developing them. This not only means researching the facts surrounding their lives, but allowing yourself to connect with them. When you do, your readers will, too.

And while you're at it, don't forget that the people you're researching can be the perfect foundation on which to base future fictional characters.

But What's A *Great* Character?

While you might expect a long and complex answer to this question, the definition is actually quite simple: a great character is remarkable, as in extraordinary, unique and worthy of notice. And what makes a character remarkable is that she is

1. *consistent*
2. *believable*
3. *admirable*

When put together, these attributes give readers what they most want, a fascinating character they can trust.

Consistent

You might think consistency means acting in a predictable manner. Yet people often act in odd, hypocritical ways. Since we can't accuse them of being created by bad writers, what gives?

What gives is that consistency stems not from people's actions, but from the basic rules underlying their belief systems. If we believe people are acting hypocritically, it's usually because we don't understand their belief systems. If we did, we'd find their actions consistent with the rules by which they govern themselves. Sometimes these rules make sense and sometimes they don't, just as sometimes people are aware of the rules by which they operate and sometimes they're not. Whatever the case, people tend to remain true to those beliefs, thus guaranteeing consistency that is often very strange.

By understanding your characters' belief systems, you'll know how they'll act in any given situation. This is a tremendously powerful concept in that as long as we know what defines our characters, we can make them do all sorts of absurd and marvelous things without any loss of credibility among readers.

Fiction Example:

Captain Jack Aubrey is the main character in *Master and Commander*, one of Patrick O'Brian's British naval novels from the Aubrey/Maturin series set during the Napoleonic Wars. Something of a rogue, Aubrey believes in both personal ambition and loyalty as defined by the complex naval code of honor. Therefore, so long as his actions stem from those beliefs, his behavior can span everything from acts of trickery, shame, ridicule and love without causing readers to doubt his consistency.

Having mentioned earlier that nonfiction characters can be the basis for fictional characters, it should be noted that Aubrey is one such example. The character was inspired by Thomas Cochrane, the tenth Earl of Dundonald who began his career as a midshipman and wound up an admiral in the British Navy after many brilliant exploits at sea and stints commanding the Chilean, Brazilian and Greek navies.

Nonfiction Example:

In her memoir *Cottage for Sale: A Woman Moves a House to Make a Home*, Cape Cod resident Kate Whouley explains how and why she bought a tiny beach vacation cottage to attach to her small hillside home.

Whouley hooks readers immediately by telling them one of the basic rules by which she lives: that reading about and owning things once owned by others feeds her soul and imagination. "The classified ads, for me, are like reading stories, or maybe like reading the skeletons of stories, waiting for me to invent their skin." Every action Whouley relates thereafter ties directly back to that preference of story over newness and convenience, which makes her consistent, so that a story about something as potentially mundane as a cottage relocation becomes a fascinating life adventure.

Believable

If grounding characters in a basic belief system makes them consistent, then matching the rest of them — actions, voice, dress and knowledge — to those beliefs makes them believable. In other words, a character's interior should match his exterior. While this should be obvious, writers often mismatch the two.

Say we create a teen-aged graffiti punk who believes it's his job to tweak society's sense of propriety as a hedge against widespread apathy, then go on to describe how he pines for the cutest girl in school, wishes he could be part of a cool group and studies hard so he won't get bad grades. Is this character believable? No, because his conformist exterior doesn't match the nonconformist interior we first described.

Now imagine the character wears bow ties instead of the usual T-shirt and jeans. He excels in art, listens to German grunge bands and knows more about the cruising habits of police cars than about sports, girls and teen celebrities put together. Is this a character readers can believe in? No question.

Fiction Example:

Christopher in Mark Haddon's *The Curious Incident of the Dog in the Night-Time* is an autistic teenager who overcomes his many compulsions and fears to solve a small mystery and deal with the resulting crisis. Christopher's consistency is grounded in an intense desire to be left alone so he can do math, his favorite activity. Although Christopher pushes himself far beyond his own limits, his exterior stays true to his militantly routine, extremely anti-touchy-feely interior.

Nonfiction Example:

Starting Right With Turkeys by G. T. Klein, published in 1946, is a matter-of-fact resource about how to run a turkey farm, from selecting, growing and killing turkeys to recordkeeping. After establishing himself as an expert, Klein goes on to impart knowledge and employ the terminology to match his claim. "The first two weeks of brooding can be in batteries or home-constructed brooders even though these provide no sunshine and only give poults limited room for exercise." Instead of using *incubator*, he uses b*rooder*. Instead of calling them *baby turkeys*, they're *poults*. Is this a man we can trust to tell us why "it is most unwise" to attempt raising turkeys in too little square footage? Right on.

Admirable

We often use the term likeable when recalling our favorite characters. Yet on closer inspection, the characters are not so much likeable as admirable for possessing an exceptional quality, skill, talent or drive.

The key word here is *exceptional*. People are as riveted by discovering the extraordinary as they are by finding buried treasure, whether it is actual wealth or something as illusive as truth and beauty.

Like buried treasure, extraordinary qualities lay hidden in places that can only be found when characters take action, the more dangerous and difficult the better. And it's that action — that search — that makes readers so ravenous for more.

Nonfiction Example:

While Wolfgang Amadeus Mozart's genius for composition became apparent at an early age, would he be famous today if he hadn't liked music? Probably not, because as we all know, simply possessing a marvelous talent isn't enough; you've got to have a burning desire to develop it. So while Mozart was born with an awesome ability, we could argue that his truly exceptional ability was in embracing and developing his gift to the highest degree. Is that kind of drive admirable? Absolutely.

Fiction Example:

A privileged child in pre-Civil War Georgia, there's not much to like about Scarlett O'Hara in Margaret Mitchell's *Gone With the Wind*. The protagonist is spoiled, selfish, manipulative and cruel. So what makes her a fantastic character? Her indomitable will to survive. This woman has such a strong sense of self-preservation that she turns into a world-class fighter when she's given cause to bare her claws. Is that an admirable quality? You bet.

Types of Characters

Now it's time to look at the various types of characters and their general purposes, or functions, which will accomplish two things:

1. Force you to decide who the story is really about

2. Clarify who, among all the people connected to your main character, plays an important part in the story

Protagonist

Definition: a main character around which the story revolves.

Purpose: to take readers on a journey in which the character experiences a personal change.

The protagonist's physical and mental journey should be the focal point of the story.

Consider the sinking of the Titanic in 1912. If the luxury liner had been largely uninhabited when it sank, the incident would have been a small note in history. What makes the story so riveting were the passengers, who, over the course of less than three hours, changed from regular people to terrified human beings who took extreme actions ranging from the brave to the cowardly. By following specific people to the point of that transformation, many moviemakers and authors have conveyed the depth of the tragedy.

While most authors have only one protagonist, you could choose several, as Amy Tan did in *The Joy Luck Club*, a novel that follows the lives of four Chinese women and their Chinese-American daughters. Keep in mind that the more protagonists you have, the more challenging it is to fully develop each and illustrate their respective journeys.

One of the most popular methods of telling the protagonist's story is through the *first-person point of view* in which the protagonist speaks directly to the reader (i.e., "I'm going to tell you my story."). Another favorite is to tell the story through the protagonist's eyes via an unnamed narrator, a strategy known as the *third-person limited point of view* (i.e., "Tom looked down, unable to endure her stare. Then Tom…").

You can also have the unnamed narrator explain the thoughts and feelings of more than one character, which is called the *third-person omniscient point of view* (i.e., "Lisa didn't want to say anything, nor did Steve, and George decided he would go along with them…").

Lastly, the *third-person objective point of view* means the unnamed narrator simply reports on what's seen and heard, rather than what the characters think and feel (i.e., "After looking at one another for a long moment, Harold gestured for Joan to sit.")

Fiction Example:

Ralph, the protagonist in *Lord of the Flies* by William Golding, is one of many schoolboys stranded on a deserted island after their plane crashes during World War II. Although Ralph begins as the leader of the group, he slowly loses out to the antagonist, who eventually hunts him down. "Then Ralph was running beneath trees, with the grumble of the forest explained. They had smoked him out and set the island on fire." When written as such, we're not only allowed to see the action through the protagonist's eyes, but also hear his thoughts and experience his feelings.

While including the perspectives of several other characters, Golding is careful to tell most of the story through Ralph as he journeys from cocky schoolboy to terrified human fleeing a hell of barbarism.

Nonfiction Example:

In *The Stranger Beside Me*, true crime writer Ann Rule gives a first-person account of meeting and working with Ted Bundy, who was executed in 1989 for the murder of a 13-year-old Florida girl, though he was believed to have killed more than 36 young women.

While Bundy is the selling point of the book, Rule is the protagonist. Over the course of the book, she transforms from a fledgling crime writer to a woman who must confront the creepy fact that she knows, likes, and once worked at a volunteer crisis center with a man who kills women for fun. At first unable to accept the possibility of his guilt, Rule goes to visit him in prison in 1976, after which she has a terrible dream where she saves an injured infant, only to see she's actually rescued a demon that then bites her. "I did not have to be a Freudian scholar to understand my dream; it was all too clear. Had I been trying to save a monster, trying to protect something or someone who was too dangerous and evil to survive?"

Rule said she began writing the book from the third-person omniscient point of view, which kept a distance between her and Bundy. But she soon realized she played a key role in the story. "After writing 100 pages or more, I realized it wasn't working and that I needed to tell about my history with Bundy from the first person. So I scrapped what I had written so far, and started over."

Antagonist

Definition: a character who tests and challenges the protagonist.

Purpose: to act as a roadblock on the protagonist's journey, thus causing tension that forces the protagonist to make choices and ultimately, change.

While it might be tempting to think of the antagonist as a black-caped, mustachioed villain who's bad to the core, great antagonists are rarely that cliché. In fact, they're not necessarily evil at all, and especially not in the black and white way most of us define evil, which is to purposely harm others for the fun or intrigue of it.

Then why do antagonists get a bad rap? Because their job is to oppose the protagonist.

Picture our protagonist, a grubby little boy who's glaring at his mother. He doesn't want to take a bath but she's determined to make him take one, which makes her the antagonist. Does her desire to get him clean make her evil? Of course not.

There can be any number of reasons for an antagonist's opposition: a radically different belief system, bad habits formed during an unfortunate upbringing, divergent goals. Whatever the reason, what's most important is that the opposition be strong enough to push the protagonist into a corner.

Fiction Example:

Stargirl Caraway in the young adult novel *Stargirl* by Jerry Spinelli is a new arrival at an Arizona high school. A fantastic free-thinking spirit, she wears costumes to school and bursts into song whenever she feels like it, which earns her a reputation as a weirdo. Yet 16-year-old Leo Borlock, the protagonist, finds her fascinating and disturbing. He longs to experience her freedom, yet fears nonconformity. Stargirl forces Leo to change not by being evil, but simply by being herself.

Nonfiction Example:

In *All Brave Sailors: The Sinking of the Anglo-Saxon, August 21, 1940*, author J. Revell Carr tells a fascinating World War II maritime story involving Hellmuth von Ruckteschell. The captain of a German raider ship, he obliterated a British merchant ship off the African coast and then fired upon two lifeboats filled with survivors, killing all.

Seven men escaped in a third boat, though ultimately only two survived a terrible 70 days at sea.

Carr does a wonderful job of portraying the German captain as a working class guy who happens to be an exceptionally successful raider captain. A religious man, Ruckteschell's highest duty is first to God, then country, which he serves to his utmost ability despite severe mood swings and blinding, stress-related headaches. Eccentric? Yes. Intimidated by his own officers? Yes. Blinded by patriotism, duty and ambition? All yes. But evil?

If you apply the broadest definition of the word — to cause harm — then yes. Then again, under that definition, most of us would be considered evil at some point or other. Yet we would probably argue that our actions were necessary and based on higher virtues like patriotism or love and if anything bad happened as a result, it's an unfortunate byproduct. The same could be said for Ruckteschell, who stayed true to his belief system of God first and country second. He did everything in his power to help his country win, even if it meant breaking the rules. Does that make Ruckteschell a monster, a hero, or a man who made a tragic decision?

Other Examples:

While most stories have one definite, flesh and blood antagonist like Ruckteschell, your antagonist could be dead, which is the case in *Rebecca*, Daphne du Maurier's classic novel about a naïve young English woman who marries a wealthy older man.

As soon as the new mistress arrives at the fabulous Manderly estate, she's haunted by the legacy of Rebecca, her husband's glamorous former wife who drowned under mysterious circumstances. Her presence is so overwhelming — the exquisite décor, the abundance of flowers, the elegant monogram on her stationary — that the ghost of Rebecca seems to laugh scornfully at the protagonist and her common ways.

Antagonists can also be a group of people, such as the dueling gangs in the musical *West Side Story*; a natural phenomenon like the hurricane featured in Sebastian Junger's nonfiction thriller, *The Perfect Storm: A True Story of Men Against the Sea*; and even an object, such as the murderous car in Stephen King's *Christine*.

Catalyst

Definition: a character who precipitates change.

Purpose: to add tension by escalating change either in the character and/or the plot.

If the tension between the antagonist and protagonist is a powder keg, the catalyst is the spark that lights the fuse.

Consider a protagonist and antagonist in hand-to-hand combat. The catalyst arrives and throws a gun, which lands squarely between the two fighters. The action jumps the scene from an altercation with injuries to one that might now result in death, and who will be the victor?

The catalyst can be a separate character or combined with the antagonist into one character who not only blocks the protagonist, but also pushes him over the edge.

The catalyst can also be a prominent character in the book or featured only once. Lastly, the catalyst can consciously or unconsciously instigate a problem, or simply be an unwitting bystander like the unlucky woman who walks in just as a desperate bank robber needs a hostage.

Fiction Example:

The character of Tybalt in William Shakespeare's *Romeo and Juliet* acts as a catalyst by killing Romeo's friend. In turn, Romeo kills Tybalt and is thrown out of town. Without Tybalt, Romeo would never be banished, which means there would be no chance for miscommunication between him and Juliet, which means there would be no story.

Nonfiction Example:

W. Mark Felt, former assistant director of the FBI, proved himself a catalyst when he stepped forward as the mysterious Deep Throat to provide Washington Post reporters with inside information following the burglary of the Democratic National Committee offices in the Watergate office complex in Washington, D.C., in 1972. Eventually traced back to President Richard Nixon, the event led to his resignation in 1974. Had Felt not taken action, the administration's illegal dealings may have remained buried beneath unsubstantiated accusations and innuendo.

Support

Definition: a character who supports the protagonist, either wittingly or unwittingly.

Purpose: to help the protagonist complete her journey.

Support characters are often the protagonist's friendly sidekick who helps by offering advice, inspiration, information or a combination thereof. But support characters can also be the opposite, abrasive prodders who needle the protagonist toward action.

Either way, support characters help the protagonist progress on her journey. They are usually memorable, mentioned more than once and given names.

Fiction Example:

One of the most famous sidekicks in literary history is Dr. Watson, the loyal friend and colleague of the renowned fictional sleuth, Sherlock Holmes, created by Sir Arthur Conan Doyle. Besides being a calm friend who balances Holmes' abrupt, high-energy persona, Watson acts as the all-important sounding board off of which Holmes bounces his whodunit theories. Watson even helps Holmes test those theories by performing errands, carrying out experiments and offering professional advice.

Nonfiction Example:

The Conquest of Everest by Sir John Hunt is the fascinating account of the first successful attempt to climb Mount Everest. Although Hunt organized the expedition, the two men who finally reached the summit on May 29, 1953, were New Zealander Sir Edmund Hillary and Nepalese climber Tenzing Norgay. While focusing more on Hilary, Hunt does a wonderful job of portraying Norgay as an extremely important support character who directly adds to the expedition's success due to his strength, expertise and enthusiasm.

Side

Definition: a peripheral character.

Purpose: to set the tone of a scene; populate locales; add color; increase tension.

Side characters have a peripheral role in a story, and for that reason are often considered unnecessary clutter to be cut during editing. Yet side characters can be one of the most effective ways to sharpen a scene and make it real.

For example, we could write, "After stepping off the bus with his suitcase, Billy Bob stood watching the city people for awhile." Or we could write this: "After stepping off the bus with his suitcase, Billy Bob's eyes landed on a tall blond man wearing a lime green skirt and pink pumps. Startled by rapid fire, as if from a machine gun, Billy Bob whipped around to see a lean black man bared to the waist, tap dancing on a large plank of wood. Tourists, dressed in fleece against the cold salt air, stood watching while eating clam chowder from sourdough bread bowls."

What did the second description tell us that the first didn't? Everything. Specifically, that the newly-arrived man is in a city that's both colorful and liberal, given the cross dresser, and somewhat big and famous, given the tourists. The city is located next to an ocean, since people are dressed against the cold salt air and eat clam chowder. We've also conveyed the mood of the locale, in that people are relaxed as they eat and watch a street performer.

By simply describing real people — where they are, what they're doing, what they're wearing, how they're reacting to one another — you can immediately convey everything about a scene, from its location to the current emotional atmosphere, whether tense, curious or excited.

Nonfiction Example:

Long-distance swimmer Lynne Cox used side characters to great effect in her memoir *Swimming to Antarctica: Tales of a Long-Distance Swimmer*.

After arriving in Egypt in 1974 for a competition in the Nile, Cox describes what she sees from her hotel room: the sight and sound of women hawking pita from the back of wagons as children swat flies away from the bread; an odd array of both Western and Middle Eastern dress; pedestrians attempting to cross the street amid a chaotic stream of vehicles.

She also uses side characters to add humor, like the Egyptian journalist who comes to her room on the pretense of an interview. After a few minutes, however, he gets up and closes her door. Feeling uncomfortable, Cox opens it again. The man reaches out and touches her arm, remarking on her tight muscles. Then he offers to give her a massage, proclaims himself a Christian and tells her that in three years he will speak to Cox's father. When Cox asks why, the man says to discuss marriage, an offer Cox politely, but firmly, declines.

It's a very funny scene that Cox could have left out. But its inclusion illustrated a cultural gap between herself — a naïve young American girl — and a Middle Eastern man.

Alternately, side characters can add tension. For example, the presence of a man, his face in shadow as he leans against a light pole on a barren city street, definitely creates a sense of foreboding.

Character Bill of Rights

Now that we understand the types of characters and how they can help us tell our stories, it's time to make a commitment to every character we create. Namely, we'll create all characters, no matter how central or peripheral, with equal enthusiasm and without taint of cliché. Furthermore, although more central characters will take longer to develop — anywhere from days to years — lesser characters can and should be guaranteed believability and purpose. Lastly, nonfiction characters should be as carefully considered and developed as their fictional brethren with the aim of adding to the protagonist's journey instead of detracting from it.

Character Study 1

To illustrate what we learn in each chapter, we'll develop a character together over the course of the book. Since most authors are interested in developing protagonists for book-length projects, whether plays, memoirs, mysteries or otherwise, we'll make our character a protagonist in a novel and specifically, a woman in her early thirties. Though she doesn't know it yet, she'll have to endure grueling physical, mental and emotional hardship.

Your Character

Exercise 1: The Introduction

Create a file for your project. This can be a computer file, a substantial notebook or even a filing cabinet. Now create your file's first document, titled *Characters*.

Use the document to list the types of characters you'll need in your story and their general purposes. Beside each, list the character's primary function along with any brief, basic information about his gender and approximate age.

Using our character as an example, this is what the document might look like:

Characters

1. Protagonist: (purpose: to go on a journey) a woman in her early thirties

2. Antagonist: (purpose: push protagonist toward conflict) the protagonist's mother

3. Catalyst: (increase tension) Aboriginal man, early sixties

4. Support: (purpose: to urge the protagonist on) protagonist's friend at work

5. Side: (purpose: add color, tension, set scene) boyfriend, people at work, at airport, on plane

Keep your thinking loose and relaxed. List as many characters as you think you'll need since you can always cut characters later if they prove unnecessary.

When done, choose one character to develop from here on out so you can experience the process from beginning to end. You can then go back and develop your other characters.

After choosing the character you'll work on, open your project file and create a file specifically for the character. Using an appropriate title, such as *Protagonist*, this is where you'll store all the documents related to her growth.

Now that you're all set, the hunt begins.

Chapter 2
Gathering Ideas

When a master gardener undertakes a project, she doesn't buy whatever strikes her fancy and plant it in random spots. She takes time to consult design books; makes a careful study of the garden's location, physical properties and weather patterns; and even visits other gardens for inspiration. She knows the more information and ideas she gathers, the better chance she'll have of creating a successful garden.

Similarly, we'll gather ideas about who our characters can become, from physical characteristics to dispositions. And there's no better way to collect data than by taking a much closer look at everyone and everything around us. In fact, it's only by becoming genuinely interested in other people and their lives that we'll learn to think more deeply about the minute details that could make our characters unique. While we're at it, we'll gather raw material for other characters while studying those who populate the places we'll describe in our stories.

So grab a notebook, laptop, sound recorder, camera or a combination thereof and set out to discover all the small things you've never noticed before. Be sure to visit a variety of public areas — coffee shops, parks, festivals, sporting events, dog tracks, main streets, etc. — at different times of the day and even during different seasons. The number and type of people populating Chicago's financial district on a sunny weekday in the summer, for example, is very different than on an early Saturday morning in December.

Upon Closer Inspection

Being writers interested in the human condition, we're probably more observant than most people. Yet that's not good enough. We have to imagine ourselves entering a fabulous garden on a serious mission to study life up close. Instead of bringing a cheap magnifying glass, we'll tote a heavy duty one that will dramatically increase the magnification of everything around us, bringing minute details — shapes, colorations, patterns — into sharp focus. While we're at it, we'll open all of our senses to the same level of magnification.

Look

The easiest and most obvious way to study people is by looking at them. When you do, note their body types, coloring, dress and unusual markings. Are they broad in the shoulders, thick around the ankles, graced with jutting chins? Do they always have a high flush to their cheeks? How close together are that child's eyes? What's the shape of that old man's face? Describe the tattoo on the back of the short man's hairy calf. Note the woman's white bobby socks, black high heels and pink mini skirt. And how long, exactly, is the hair growing from the mole on the man's chin?

Once you've taken a good look at skin colors, clothes, facial features, etc., progress to observing how people move. This includes their facial expressions, gestures and how they carry themselves. Have you ever met a person who emphasizes a comment by holding his hands parallel to one another, as if holding a box? How about the woman who walks chest forward as if led by the breastbone? And don't forget the man who constantly winks, making you unsure about whether he's including you in a private joke, making a play for you or just being his twitchy self.

Fiction Example:

Hana, the protagonist in *The English Patient,* is a World War II nurse who stays behind in an abandoned Italian villa to care for a severely burned man who tells her his life story. Rather than describe the man in blunt and general terms, author Michael Ondaatje uses deep, rich, specific details that convey not only the burned man's physical appearance, but also his agony. "She has nursed him for months and knows his body well, the penis sleeping like a sea horse, the thin tight hips... She loves the hollow below the lowest rib, its cliff of skin... Reaching his shoulders, she blows cool air onto his neck... He turns his dark face with its grey eyes toward her."

Nonfiction Example:

Regarding the power of gestures and what they say about a character, consider the 9-year-old neighbor girl who befriended humor writer David Sedaris when he was a young man living in a slum apartment building. In *The Girl Next Door*, Sedaris describes how she spent long hours alone while her shrewish, hard-living bartender mother worked. At one point the girl shows Sedaris a doll that's still in its original box. The mother apparently gave her daughter the doll and then forbade her to play with it.

Sedaris could have told readers that though tempted to open the box, the girl didn't for fear of her mother's wrath. But instead he uses a hand gesture to convey the sentiment. "She would trace her finger along the outside of the box, tempting herself, but never once did I see her lift the lid."

Listen

Once you've taken in as many details as possible with your eyes, it's time to close them and use your ears. By listening to the sounds people make, either intentionally or unintentionally, you'll begin to understand how sound can convey information subtly and so allow readers to discover the character on their own.

Specifically, the sounds people make give clues about where they were born, their general disposition and their present physical, emotional and mental state. A person who sighs fast once, with a harsh hissing undertone, could be very annoyed, whereas a person who sighs slowly while gazing at nothing in particular could be melancholy.

With that in mind, listen to how people clear their throats and what noises they make when nervous. When they speak, note the tone of their voice. Is it high, low, intense, whispery, urgent, bored? What kind of accent do people have? Do they keep their mouths mostly closed as in a Minnesotan accent? Do they come from Boston and so drop the "R" in words so that "before" becomes "befaw"? If they have a foreign accent you can't identify, describe it. Does it sound like they're slurping spaghetti, biting air, chewing their cud?

Fiction Example:

Speak the following quote aloud and listen to the wonderful dialect Annie Proulx assigns to Uncle Nolan in *The Shipping News*. An old man who lives in a shack in Newfoundland, he's rescued from neglect and starvation by Quoyle, the protagonist, who later goes to visit the old man in a care facility. And how is Uncle Nolan doing? "Oh! Wunnerful! Wunnerful food! They's 'ot rainbaths out of the ceiling, my son, oh, like white silk, the soap she foams up in you 'and."

Nonfiction Example:

Mark Twain uses sound to marvelous effect in an essay titled *Corn-pone Opinions* when describing a young black slave who would stand atop a woodpile behind his master's house and preach to a young and impressed Twain. "He interrupted his preaching, now and then, to saw a stick of wood; but the sawing was a pretense — he did it with his mouth; exactly imitating the sound the bucksaw makes in shrieking its way through the wood. But it served its purpose; it kept his master from coming out to see how the work was getting along."

Smell

You should also pick up information via your nose even if the idea at first seems repugnant. Like visual and audible details, scents can tell an enormous amount about characters; their personal hygiene habits, food preferences, what they do for a living, problems they may have. If they smell like cigarettes, they probably smoke. If their breath always smells like cumin and curry, maybe they eat a lot of Indian food. If they smell of Neoprene and saltwater, they could be commercial divers.

Fiction Example:

Returning to Uncle Nolan in *The Shipping News*, this is what Quoyle finds when he walks into the old man's shack and finds him near death: "The stink gagging. The old man too weak or befuddled to get to the outhouse. A skeleton trembled before them."

Nonfiction Example:

In *Disturbed Ground*, Carla Norton describes Dorothea Puente, a woman who has everyone convinced she's a sweet old lady who operates a boarding house for the downtrodden in Sacramento, CA. Suspicious that Puente is out to steal her boarders' Social Security checks, Ben Johnson visits. While he doesn't find his friend, Bert, he does tour the well-kept home. But what really convinces him of Puente's integrity is the savory smell of pot roast wafting through the house.

He leaves, unaware of the dead bodies buried in Puente's front yard.

Learn

Besides studying people from a distance, it's necessary to talk to them, because everyone — *everyone* — has something to teach. Specifically, choose people similar to the characters you have in mind. Strike up a conversation and keep talking until you understand their likes, dislikes, viewpoints, expertise and logic. If you're planning to write a romance that takes place on a horse farm, go talk to horse people. See what they wear, how they smell, the way they handle horses and the terms they use.

Before you head out, however, understand that your attitude going into an interview determines how much information people will give you. If you advertise your strong opinions, ask questions that demonstrate your bias or show contempt for people's lifestyles and choices, the conversation will be over before it's begun.

Conversely, if you truly believe everybody does the best he can — from convicts to radicals to politicians and everyone in between — and show an honest desire to learn, you'll be amazed by how fast people open up.

If their beliefs run counter to your own, remain neutral and keep asking questions until you understand their logic, because everyone has reasons for what they do. While some people know those reasons, others might not, just as some reasons will be logical and others completely illogical. Even if they're the craziest reasons you've ever heard, that doesn't mean they're invalid or useless. To the contrary, such flawed thinking can illustrate their belief system and in turn make them more human. Consider the autobiography of Georgia Sothern, a poor southern girl who, during the Great Depression, became a stripper at the tender age of 13. Despite the lewd nature of the business, she says she never played hanky-panky.

Although hard to believe, her claim clearly conveys a strong need to portray herself as a lady in a very bawdy industry. That vulnerability allows readers to sympathize with Sothern.

Lastly, remember that what you learn from other people could be the very information necessary for making your character believable and unique. In exchange, you should be courteous and allow them the chance to be understood.

Think

After compiling a mountain of information, it's imperative to think about what you've learned in order to understand what details can make your character live and breathe.

Besides turning over facts and images, imagine what it might be like to actually be the people you've observed. Who do they go home to at night? Why do they present the public image they do? What secrets might they have? What did the shape of her eyes remind you of? And when he looked at you, how did you feel?

This guessing game — of what might be true about a person based on the information you have — is called extrapolation. It's an invaluable exercise that opens your mind to new possibilities, weens you away from thinking of everyone and everything in relation to yourself, and helps you to grow the feelings from which your own characters will sprout, a process we'll discuss more in *Chapter 6, Growing Your Character*.

Minutia Diary

For an idea of how to record information and extrapolate about people's lives, here are a few examples from my document of details, which I call my *Minutia Diary*:

— a guy who hangs up his dental floss to dry so he can re-use it (either endures severe financial deprivation or is neurotic)

— a woman who likes burned cookies for the combination of sweet and bitter (likes life like that, too, the bitter making the sweet sweeter)

— an older man who likes to say, "He's all hat and no cattle." (routinely appraises people to determine if they're full of cow dung)

Get Organized

While it's admirable to amass hundreds of sensory details with which to work, such a load can be overwhelming. To keep from getting buried, get organized by opening your character's file and creating a document titled *Details* and list all your observations according to whatever system helps you easily find what you want. Then whenever you use a detail in your story, make a note on this worksheet to keep from using the same detail twice.

An example of such organization looks like this:

Details

Colors

— light tan face powder that's melted and congealed in the cracks of her face

Gestures

— whenever he sits, he puts his elbows on the table and touches the tips of his fingers together

— when she's stressed, she presses her right middle
finger between her eyes for about 10 seconds

Smells

— a very light orange-ginger smell on her skin, like
from the oil in an expensive body wash

— I rubbed the stem of a lavender plant and it was
like a little cloud of lavender exploded around me,
the sharp scent overwhelming

If you don't have time to organize your notes, highlight the most
fascinating details, using different colors to delineate between various
categories, such as pink for funny details, red for unusual hairstyles
and yellow for the way people talk.

While such organization may seem like busywork, it will help you
access information quickly while weeding out mediocre data from the
exceptional details.

Character Study 2

In the last chapter we decided to grow a female protagonist in her
thirties. Using an observation from our list, we'll assign her a unique
pattern of movement: when looking around, she quickly shifts her
face from one person to the next in an abrupt, almost birdlike
movement. While only one detail, it tells us she's probably a nervous
person who feels that if she lets her guard down, she might miss
something big.

Your Character

Exercise 2: Possible Attributes

Now you can do for your character what we've just done for our protagonist.

To begin, open your character's file and create a main worksheet for him and title it appropriately, such as *Protagonist's Worksheet*. Open the document and create a subheading titled "Possible Attributes." Referring to your *Details* document, list all the attributes you could apply to your character. Don't worry about quantity or quality since you can easily add details and jettison others along the way.

If you feel excitement building, you should, because you're close to the magical moment when you choose the seed from which your character will grow. Only a little more groundwork remains.

Chapter 3
Narrowing Your Selection

Once a master gardener has an idea of everything she'd like to include in her project, she has to narrow her focus from the whole garden to specific sections and what she'll put in each.

Similarly, now that you know what type of character you're developing and the details that can make him unique, it's time to narrow from the general to the specific.

From the General to the Specific

As you narrow from the general to the specific, your character will begin to take on a definite shape as well as depth, color and detail. At the same time, it means you'll soon have to commit to a specific location in which to plant your character. Choose carefully and your character will thrive. Choose poorly and you may have to transplant him, which is time-consuming as well as risky, there being no guarantee he'll survive the upheaval.

With that in mind, we'll begin narrowing from the character's general purpose to his specific purpose. If he's a protagonist, his general purpose is to take readers on a journey. But what's his specific purpose?

Ask the Right Question

To determine the correct answer to anything, you must first ask the correct question. In this case, if you want to know your character's specific purpose, the right question is

What, specifically, will the character have to endure over the course of the book?

Will she have to discover a cure for her strange illness before it kills her? Will he have to solve a 20-year-old mystery? Will she have to rescue hundreds of people?

When you think you've found the answer, it's time to test your thinking.

Test Your Thinking

By testing our thinking at every stage of a character's development, we force ourselves to ask whether we're making the best possible choices and if not, what will work better.

While we could simply think over our options, a better way to analyze an idea's ramifications is to employ the two-step method of 1) self-conversation and 2) the one-sentence test.

Self-conversation

Self-conversation is an internal conversation in which you hash out the logic of your ideas.

To get started, open your character's file and create a third document titled *Self-conversations*. After a brief description of the idea you're pondering, begin transcribing the ensuing internal conversation with the goal of evaluating every angle of the idea. Since no one will ever see this document, be as honest and unselfconscious as you can while not worrying about spelling, punctuation or grammar. For example:

Self-conversation

Specific purpose: If this character is an antagonist, his job is to challenge the protagonist. Specifically, he rides the protagonist hard to get results. Yet that's not specific enough. What does my character have to actually endure? Well, he has to watch the reputable police department he built crumble under allegations of corruption. That would be pretty torturous for such a proud, religious, straight-laced guy like him. Angry and stressed out, it's no wonder he's so hard on the protagonist. But would office troubles be enough to make him miserable? It could, especially if he's losing sleep over it. Yet maybe it would be more interesting if I also gave him a problem outside of work; something that could parallel the office woes and add to the stress and tension levels. As if by driving the protagonist to get results in the office, the antagonist also hopes to get the answer to his real agony. What is his real agony? Cancer? Something he did during the war that still haunts him? Being diagnosed with Alzheimer's? That's it! Because what could be worse than losing control of your empire? Losing control of your mind.

Besides clarifying ideas, self-conversation is also an effective pressure gauge that helps relieve frustration and doubt. You can even use self-conversation to talk directly to your character. Consider Halen McFee, the character from the previous example:

Self-conversation

Specific Purpose: Hey Halen, what's your specific purpose?

Do I know you? I don't think so. What's your name and why are you standing around asking stupid questions when you should be working? I didn't build this department from scratch so you could take a goddamned two-hour coffee break. Specific purpose, my ass. My specific purpose is to keep young recruits like you under control so you don't get somebody killed. Now get out of here!

While such a conversation may seem strange if you've never done it before, it's not uncommon for authors to talk to their characters. After all, which is easier, to learn about someone in another room by guessing what he's thinking, or to invite him in and ask him directly?

The One-sentence Test

When done with self-conversation, the next step is to check the solidity of your decision by employing the one-sentence test. To understand the difference between the two, think of self-conversation as a home study course and the one-sentence test as the final exam.

The trick to this final, however, is that there's only one question, and while you've got enough material to fill an essay booklet, your answer must be confined to one sentence.

Let's return to Halen McFee. If the question is, *What will this character have to endure over the course of the book?*, the one-sentence answer could be, *This character will have to endure not only the humiliation of watching what he built collapse, but the fact that he's losing control of his mind.*

Note that the sentence is short and concise. If it had turned into a long run-on sentence — an explanation rather than a simple statement — then you either don't know the character's specific purpose, or the character isn't necessary. If the former, go back to your self-conversation and keep working. If the latter, shed a brief tear and cut the character from your list. Whatever you do, don't proceed until your character's specific purpose is clear.

Fiction Example:

In Charlotte Bronte's *Jane Eyre*, published in England in 1847, the protagonist's general purpose is to take us on a journey. Specifically, Jane must survive on her own, first as an unwelcome orphan in her aunt's home, then in a forbidding boarding school and finally as a governess in a strange house.

Mrs. Fairfax, the housekeeper, is a support character. Her general purpose is to support the protagonist. Her specific purpose is to be kind to Jane and warn her away from the brooding Mr. Rochester, Jane's employer.

As the catalyst of the book, Richard Mason's general purpose is to hike the tension level. He does so by showing up on the eve of Jane and Mr. Rochester's wedding to blab Mr. Rochester's deep, dark secret.

Nonfiction Example:

In the fabulous memoir *The Liars' Club*, author Mary Karr's job as the protagonist is to take us on a journey. Her specific purpose is to survive a truly rough and tumble — not to mention bizarre and tragic — childhood, first in a hardscrabble East Texas town and then in Colorado.

Lecia, Karr's older sister, is a support character who attempts to protect Karr from physical and mental abuse by being a tough-minded realist.

Then there's Karr's mother, an alcoholic prone to severe mood swings. As the antagonist, her general purpose is to challenge Karr. Specifically, the mother behaves in erratic, often threatening, ways that keep Karr constantly off balance and exposed to abuse.

Character Study 3

Let's apply the one-sentence test to learn our character's specific purpose:

After surviving a plane crash, our character will have to survive three weeks alone in the Australian outback with almost no water.

One short sentence, yet it takes our character out of a very broad category — *people who suffer* — and places her into a specific category of *those who must survive great physical hardship in the wilds of a foreign land.*

One simple sentence, yet we can already begin to feel the heat, the desolation, the desperation.

Your Character

Exercise 3: Specific Purpose

Open your character's file and create a fourth document titled *One-sentence Test.* Under the heading of "Specific Purpose," enter the answer to what your character will have to endure over the course of the book.

For example:

One-sentence Test

Specific Purpose: My character has to deal with the hurt of being the less favored son.

Don't worry if your sentence doesn't sound all that impressive. It's meant to clarify your thinking rather than be the catchy back cover blurb meant to snare readers. Not all books are potboilers involving exotic places and high adventure. Some books revolve around quiet characters who survive an abusive upbringing, such as Dave Pelzer in his nonfiction account, *A Child Called 'It.'* On the funnier side are books like Bill Bryson's travel tale *A Walk in the Woods.* The specific purpose sentence could well be, *An out-of-shape guy must endure hiking parts of the Appalachian Trail with another out-of-shape guy.* Not exactly a grabber, yet the book became a New York Times bestseller.

Once your character's specific purpose is clear in your mind — the perfect spot chosen, the hole dug — it's time for what we've all been waiting for.

Let the planting season commence.

Part II: The Right Seed

Starting plants from seed is one of the most satisfying garden activities… Even the most expert seed starters continue to feel awed by the miracle of germination and growth — how one seed (sometimes not much bigger than a speck of dust) can become a healthy, productive plant that, in some cases, is large enough to "take over" the entire garden!

— *Gardener to Gardener Seed-Starting Primer and Almanac*, edited by Vicki Mattern, Rodale Press

Chapter 4
Planting the Right Seed

The groundwork almost done and character development set to begin in earnest, there are only two tasks that remain, yet they're undoubtedly the most pivotal: choosing and planting the right seed from which your character will grow.

Think for a moment of everything a seed suggests: a beginning, a creation, an embryo from which life springs. The seed of a character is all of those things. Yet rather than be an unfathomable mix of genetic material, the seed of a character consists of only one thing, a single detail that defines him. It's this detail that will make your character great, as in believable, consistent and admirable.

The Bad Seed: Too Many Details

If defining your character based on a particular detail seems outrageous, let's look at the traditional method of creating a character based on a dense foundation of detail such as physical features, family history, psychological bent, etc.

Imagine we're working on a character named Marco, a 43-year-old man who lives in Florida, works as a heating and air conditioning repairman and spends his hard-earned money on Cuban cigars and alimony to a German ex-wife named Gretchen. Half Italian and half Polish, Marco comes from Chicago where he learned to love beef and dislike seafood almost as much as he hates taxes. He loves baseball — and spring training in particular — which is one of the reasons he moved to Florida. He has Democratic leanings, loves routine and once a week meets some ex-military buddies. And to think this is only a fraction of the data we have about Marco.

Such a thorough profile seems to make sense, in that the better we know Marco, the better our readers will, too. To test our logic, let's apply the one-sentence test:

What defines Marco?

It's difficult to say what defines Marco because our attention is drawn in too many directions. It's like viewing a 40-acre garden and trying to decide what we like best. Though we see many nice things, there are either too many favorites to name or nothing stands out. Too many details can also bury a character, hide her motivation and lead to inconsistencies.

Bury a Character

Without one specific detail to guide us in our character's development, we'll have trouble following his lead and may get stuck, a problem commonly known as writer's block.

Or even worse, we might know our character inside and out, yet when the rejection slip comes, there's a note at the bottom saying the agent or editor couldn't connect with the character because he seemed too indistinct. *Good God*, we might think, *what more does she want?*

The answer lies in the fact that agents and editors are first and foremost readers who want to be hooked by a good story and all it promises: hours of surprise, suspense, learning and emotional involvement. The best way to hook them is to show what's most important to your character, because when they know that, they'll understand the character and be willing to ride along on his journey.

Hide Motivation

If readers don't understand your character's internal belief system, his exterior actions may seem random and nonsensical.

Think of Marco. Though buried beneath details, he comes off as more or less a nice guy. Now imagine a scene in which he's nasty to his ex-wife. While we know he has a right to be, our readers don't because we haven't told them what's most important to Marco, which is vital for interpreting his actions. All they know is that he seemed like a nice guy, but now he's acting like a jerk. Disgusted, they'll put the story down, never to pick it up again.

Lead to Inconsistencies

Amassing too many details makes it easy to lose track of what we've collected, a situation that almost guarantees some of those details will contradict one another and make our character appear inconsistent. Say we mention how Marco loves to watch spring baseball training. One detail among many, we forget it and move on. But because readers don't know what's most important to Marco, they may attempt to figure it out for themselves by attaching more significance to the detail than we intended. They may think Marco's love of spring training is a sign he's a diehard patriot with a major soft spot for America and that this attribute will play a major role in the book.

Now imagine we write a scene in which Marco takes off during spring training for a last-minute fishing and drinking weekend with his buddies. Not only will his decision puzzle readers, but his spontaneity contradicts a stated preference for routine. While the latter simply makes the character appear inconsistent, the former forces readers to conclude the spring training thing was just some throwaway detail, in which case they feel duped, the character appears shallow and we look careless.

The Defining Detail

Rather than bury your character under too many details, choose one specific detail to define your character. This detail will be the seed from which your character grows in every aspect, from physical appearance to beliefs and actions. And because everything stems from this point of origin, the defining detail is what will make your character first believable, then consistent, then admirable.

In short, choosing and planting the right defining detail is what will make your character great.

Why It's All Important

To fully understand why a defining detail works so well, consider what happens when a seed germinates. It sends down roots that hold the plant in place. Then the plant begins to grow according to its specific genetic code. Yet rather than be an exact duplicate of others within its species, the plant grows according to its unique circumstances, such as placement in the soil and exposure to the sun. And when necessary, the plant does what's necessary to survive, whether by growing thorns to protect it from predators or putting forth gorgeous, aromatic blooms that invite bees and other cross-pollinating insects.

Now apply that process to character development beginning with psychogenesis, when the character takes root. By growing according to her nature, she becomes consistent, just as reacting to her specific circumstances makes her original. Lastly, motivation allows her to do what's necessary to survive.

Psychogenesis

Psychogenesis is a medical term for the origin of why a person thinks or behaves as she does. If a person experiences a terrifying house fire when young, the event could be the origin — the psychogenesis — of a lifelong fear of fire.

A defining detail serves as a character's psychogenesis, or point of origin. When readers know the exact place from which your character grows, they'll know what's most important to your character, and in turn, what motivates him.

So rooted, the defining detail will hold your character in place no matter what weather he endures, whether hurricanes, lightning strikes or seductive breezes.

Consistency

When you know where your character comes from, you can test whether her exterior actions match her interior belief system, guaranteeing the character's consistency.

Let's say Marco's defining detail is how he felt holding a bat at 2:06 p.m. on July 10, 1975, while standing at home plate during a regional Little League championship game. The last inning with two outs and a man on second, 12-year-old Marco ignores the roar of the crowd and keeps his narrowed eyes on the pitcher. In this moment of psychogenesis, he understands what it feels like to have enough confidence to challenge even God to a game and be certain of victory.

Unfortunately Marco strikes out, which ends the game and his childhood. Yet he never gets over that feeling of glory, which is why he attends spring training. A yearly ritual, it allows him to shake off his many failures and pledge his life to reclaiming success.

Our character so rooted, we can start a self conversation to extrapolate about Marco's future behavior and test whether it's consistent with his defining detail. For example:

Self-conversation

Extrapolation: Would Marco really miss spring training to go drinking with his buddies? No Way.

Does Marco think he's better than his neighbor, who's content to be a second-rate mechanic? Very likely.

Does Marco know everything about baseball, including teams, players and odds? Probably.

Why does he know so much? Does he honestly love the game, or does he think this year his persistence will pay off when he lays his bets come opening day, the proceeds earmarked to finance his *Return to Glory?* Maybe the former, probably both, but definitely the latter.

Originality

Unearthing a character's defining detail requires us to take a much closer look at him. When we do, we begin to see what makes him different from everyone else.

When we first created Marco, he was a divorced, has-been jock who loves baseball. Nothing to differentiate him from millions of other such men, he was a cliché. As such, readers would have only stopped long enough to identify Marco as a certain type, such as a bully or blue-collar stiff — more an object than a real person — then rushed past him.

But by giving Marco a specific defining detail, we made him original. A hopeful boy who grows into a down-on-his luck man, Marco refuses to give up on regaining the glory he felt while playing baseball one summer day when he was 12. He could be a neighbor, uncle or family friend, which is exactly the kind of connection that hooks readers.

But what about famous characters like Count Olaf in the *Series of Unfortunate Events* books by Daniel Handler, a.k.a. Lemony Snicket? Out to steal an inheritance from three orphans, Count Olaf is a stereotypical villain, so how can he be a great character? Because he possesses a defining detail that lifts him above cliché. Not simply a master of disguise, he has an almost otherworldly ability to make himself into characters the children don't recognize until it's almost too late.

Great defining details can also save side characters from cliché. While you won't spend as much time developing them as you will main characters, it doesn't take much effort to lift side characters out of cliché.

Consider a stereotypical gorgeous, but snotty, cheerleader who's making life hell for some less than beautiful girl. What detail could we use to cancel this cliché? How about every Wednesday she wears a black T-shirt with huge white lettering that says, *Leukemia sucks.*

If you find yourself wondering whether she or someone she knows has the disease, the detail has achieved its goal of making us curious to learn more about her.

Motivation

Motivation is what propels a character to act. That action then moves the story along. Therefore, if we want our story to move, we'd better know our character's motivation.

To make the connection absolutely clear:

Motivation = action

No motivation = no action

Say we go to work (the action) because we want to earn money (the reason). Or we get married (the action) because we want to love and be loved (the reason). Or we indulge in dangerous activities like skydiving (the action) because the resulting adrenaline rush makes us feel good (the reason). Sometimes we're aware of these motivations and sometimes we're not.

Although the reasons we do things are numerous, most motivations stem from a 1) want, 2) need, or 3) fear. Take exercise. Some of us work out regularly so we'll look nice and feel good (a want). Some of us do it because we have to for health reasons, like lowering a high cholesterol level (a need). And some exercise for fear of what will happen if they don't (a fear).

While it helps to know where motivations come from in general, we also need to know our character's specific motivation, so where do we look? At the defining detail, which points directly to a character's motivation.

Consider Marco. If he's defined by a treasured memory of glory, he's highly motivated to reclaim that glory. He wants it. He needs it. He fears what will happen if he doesn't get it.

Why It Must Be Specific

Imagine looking out over that 40-acre garden again. Your eyes land on a group of indistinct yellow flowers. Walking closer, you notice hummingbirds flitting in and out among them. Curious to understand why, you bring your face close to a single flower and notice the seahorse-shaped bloom, the streak of crimson like a drop of spilled wine and the light scent of honey. Now you understand the flower's appeal. That's why defining details should be as specific as possible, because it's only at such close proximity that readers will understand what makes your character unique.

To make your character's detail specific, start with something general — a facial scar, a childhood incident, etc. — and keep asking questions until you can picture the character so clearly you can actually see, feel, hear, touch and smell him. For example:

The woman's eyes are blue. (What kind of blue?)

The woman's eyes are blue as water. (What kind of water?)

The woman's eyes are the color of shallow water.
  (Lake water? River water?)

The woman's eyes are blue as the white sand shallows
  off an almost deserted beach. (A beach in the Aleutian
  Islands? On Cape Cod?)

The woman's eyes are blue as the white sand shallows
  off an almost deserted beach along the Sea of Cortez
  where we met one August day, the white sun high and
  hot, the breeze no more than a faint breath.

Can we now see the color of this woman's half-closed eyes as she considers us one hot afternoon, the blue-green sea just beyond? Definitely.

And so the woman's defining detail emerges, her essence depicted by the look and feel of a color; hushed, languid, exotic.

Where to Find It

Fortunately the world abounds with specific details by which to define our characters. Unfortunately, the volume can be overwhelming. To make the task simpler, start by searching a particular category of detail, and if you don't find what you're looking for, move on to the next. The following are rich sources from which to choose.

An Incident

A great place to find a defining detail is in an incident, as we did with Marco. Rather than be just any incident, however, it should be life-altering, in that the world looks different from that moment on.

Consider those who turned on their radios on Dec. 7, 1941, and heard the news of Japan's attack on Pearl Harbor in which 1,177 American servicemen died within a few hours. Such people inevitably recall how the world seemed to change in that moment, life forever split into *before the war* and *after the war*. That's because such life-altering incidents cause profound internal shifts within us that lead to psychogenesis, or the origin of new behaviors. These incidents are usually dramatic, emotional and highly memorable. They can be joyous, such as when we realize we're in love, or tragic, as when people suffer crippling accidents. They can revolve around events that are witnessed by and affect a large number of people or those experienced by only one person.

Defining incidents can stem from many sources, such as an embarrassment, habit, mistake, achievement, consequence or even conscious choice. An example of the last is when Dr. Jeffrey Wigand decided to blow the whistle on corporate corruption at Brown & Williamson Tobacco Corp. in 1995, a harrowing experience chronicled in the movie *The Insider.*

Whatever the source, defining moments are important enough that our characters should clearly remember the scene — the time of day, what they wore, who was present, etc. — as well as how they felt in that moment. Utterly lonely, angry enough to kill, or like Marco, absolutely certain of victory.

Fiction Example:

In *Ender's Game*, Orson Scott Card's famous science fiction tale, earth is on the brink of destruction due to a war with an alien race. Desperate, world leaders resort to electronically monitoring children in the hope of finding a genius who can win the war. Enter Andrew Wiggin, nicknamed Ender by his sister.

A 6-year-old boy, Ender is being tormented by a school bully. Ender knows it's leading to a fight and when it does, he has to win or the taunting will only get more vicious. So when the bully instigates the fated confrontation, Ender beats his opponent so badly the boy dies. Though Ender is never told of the boy's death, he's smart enough to suspect what happened and be horrified.

One incident, yet it illustrates Ender's defining detail, a rare mix of compassion and brutality, the reason he's eventually chosen as *The One*.

Now knowing the protagonist's defining detail, we also know his motivation: to survive Battle School without succumbing to the seductive power that turns a good person brutal.

Nonfiction Example:

A young investment banker, Trisha Meili was out running in New York City's Central Park on an April evening in 1989 when she was raped and beaten so brutally her case garnered national outrage. Left in a coma with 75 percent blood loss, Meili nonetheless survived, though with permanent physical and cognitive injuries.

Rather than succumb to the horror of what happened to her, Meili slowly recuperated and wrote *I Am the Central Park Jogger: A Story of Hope and Possibility* as a way to inspire others to persevere through seemingly insurmountable challenges.

Defined by the feeling she's not living up to her true potential, she's highly motivated to overachieve and so prove her worth.

A Prominent Physical Characteristic

If you choose a prominent physical attribute to define your character, it should strongly impact how your character views the world and vice versa. Think of 1930s-1950s movie star maven and pinup girl Betty Grable. Her shapely legs were insured by 20th Century Fox for a million dollars, a fact that almost certainly affected the way she moved, what she wore and what reactions she expected from others. In turn, her many fans expected her to look and act like a famous sex kitten.

While we can assume having one's legs insured for a cool million is an advantageous physical characteristic — akin to Chinese basketball player Yao Ming's 7-foot, 5-inch frame — prominent physical attributes can also be disadvantageous. Think buckteeth, obnoxiously red hair or comically bowed legs.

When considering physical features, choose one you can vividly imagine and convincingly portray. Just saying your character is almost 8 feet tall isn't enough. You have to imagine how his height makes him unique. Do people stare at him wherever he goes? What junk does he see stashed in high locations most people can't see?

If it's hard to understand the full ramifications of your character's attribute, try simulating the physical characteristic if it's safe to do so. If your character is blind, you could, with the help of an assistant entrusted to protect you, blindfold yourself for a day. Or think of John Howard Griffin, a white Texan who, in 1959, dyed his skin black and went to live in New Orleans so he could realistically chronicle his treatment as a black man, which he did in *Black Like Me*.

Fiction Example:

One of the most famous prominent physical characteristics in literary history is Cyrano de Bergerac's extraordinarily big nose. Based on a real person, Cyrano is defined by a nose so big it bars him from publicly stating his love for Roxanne. Motivated to mask his passion, he secretly woos the fair maiden through letters he writes under another man's name.

Nonfiction Example:

Many inspirational articles, books and other nonfiction works revolve around characters whose defining details stem from prominent physical attributes in general and physical impairments in particular. Consider *Wheelchair Around the World*, Patrick D. Simpson's account of his and his wheelchair-bound wife's travels abroad. Defined by a burning desire to travel, this couple is motivated to do whatever it takes to see the world.

An Imagined Blemish

Think of those who stoop, thinking they're too tall, or never speak up, thinking they're stupid. These are people who suffer from imagined blemishes.

The beauty of using this strategy to find a defining detail is that imagined imperfections are so common, most readers can immediately identify with characters so afflicted. And while it's often painful to watch a character wrestle nonexistent demons, it can also be fascinating and even hilarious.

Fiction Example:

Alonso Quijano, the protagonist in the 400-year-old novel *Don Quixote de la Mancha*, imagines he's a worthless man and fears dying without ever having lived. So motivated, Quijano attempts to recreate himself as a noble adventurer named Don Quixote, a knight based on characters from Quijano's beloved boyhood stories. Though ridiculed at every turn, he perseveres in his travels while guided by his tremendous imagination, which turns windmills into giants, inns into castles and common washerwomen like the local Dulcinea into grand noblewomen.

Nonfiction Example:

Shirley Ardell Mason, a.k.a Sybil Dorsett of the nonfiction book *Sybil*, is a prime example of a woman who internalized nonexistent blemishes.

Born in Minnesota in 1923, Mason suffered terrible mental and physical abuse at the hands of her mentally ill mother. While most people would have been crushed by the weight of the untrue imperfections Mason's mother heaped on her, Mason was so motivated to survive that she developed 16 personalities to cope with her mistreatment.

The Five Senses

This strategy relies on choosing a defining detail based on one of the five senses, like the woman defined by the color of her eyes. Details stemming from the five senses can be literal or simply symbolize the character's identity, or both. Besides being a color, for example, the woman's blue-green eyes are a visible manifestation of her essence. The same can be true of details spun from sounds, tastes, smells and textures. Smelling like worn shoe leather may signal a bureaucratic disposition. Or think of someone so dynamic she leaves a resonance in her wake like that of a piano after the last chord has been played.

Fiction Example:

Set in biblical times, *The Red Tent* is a story told through Dinah, a girl born to Leah and reared with the help of Rachel, Zilpah and Bilhah, the four wives of Jacob.

Rather than define Rachel in terms of her beauty, a cliché common among heroines, Dinah instead remembers Rachel as smelling like water, which conveys everything we need to know about her: that she's vital, rushing; always making waves; a cherished commodity in a desert. As such, she's motivated to embrace change and whatever life-giving force she encounters.

Nonfiction Example:

A tall, slender woman with voluminous black hair and a swanky, deep voice, my fifth-grade math teacher gave me hope that my womanhood would be as glamorous.

The first day in her class, I made sure to ask a question that would bring her close so I could get a better look at her jewelry and bask in her air of elegant importance. She walked down the aisle in her movie star way and stood slightly behind me while leaning over my shoulder to look at the problem on my worksheet. Then she spoke.

I have no idea what she said because her breath was so foul I almost passed out. Rotting, nicotined, germy clouds of gaseous pestilence. So defined by that smell, I was highly motivated to keep away from her breath.

An Object

If you're not sure a particular incident, physical characteristic or sensual trait can define your character, maybe an object will do the job. It could be a prized collection of glass figurines like that belonging to the fragile Laura in the play *The Glass Menagerie* by Tennessee Williams. Or maybe it's an obsession with steel ball bearings like the mentally unstable Captain Queeg in the novel *The Caine Mutiny* by Herman Wouk.

A defining object can also be the character's trademark, such as Sherlock Holmes' pipe and deerstalker hat, which have come to symbolize the fictional detective's precise thinking and perseverance.

Fiction Example:

In *The Ballad of the Sad Café* by Carson McCullers, the protagonist is a fiercely independent woman in a small southern town of long ago. Of all the details that make Miss Amelia unique — the slightly crossed gray eyes, gum boots, overalls and habit of feeling her well-developed arm muscles — she's best defined by the liquor she makes. Though of excellent taste, what makes the tonic profound is that it causes people to see what's deep inside them, the irony being it doesn't seem to work on Miss Amelia. Defined by an internal blindness, she continues to plow forward without seeing the disastrous ramifications of her actions.

Nonfiction Example:

Dare Wright used her childhood doll, Edith, as the main character in her bestselling children's book *The Lonely Doll*, published in 1957. Wright illustrated the book and subsequent books by arranging and photographing her doll in various positions with other characters, like a stuffed bear named Mr. Bear.

In *The Secret Life of the Lonely Doll: The Search for Dare Wright*, author Jean Nathan explains that Wright's mother gave her daughter the expensive doll as a gift when Wright was young. In turn, Wright named the doll after her mother. While it seems a sentimental gesture, the book shows how Wright's doll symbolizes who she became, a person motivated to repress her true identity in exchange for her mother's love.

What Interests You Most

When faced with a number of details that could define your character, choose what interests you most. If this strategy strikes you as presumptuous, especially when defining a nonfiction character, remember that you're writing the story, which gives you the right to depict your character as you see fit.

Fiction Example:

In *A Christmas Carol*, published in 1843, Charles Dickens seemed to have a glorious time describing what he found most interesting about Ebenezer Scrooge: a greed so insidious it froze the man from the inside out:

> *Oh! But he was a tight-fisted hand at the grind-stone, Scrooge! a squeezing, wrenching, grasping, scraping, clutching, covetous, old sinner! Hard and sharp as flint, from which no steel had ever struck out generous fire; secret, and self-contained, and solitary as an oyster. The cold within him froze his old features, nipped his pointed nose, shriveled his cheek, stiffened his gait; made his eyes red, his thin lips blue; and spoke out shrewdly in his grating voice. A frosty rime was on his head, and on his eyebrows, and his wiry chin. He carried his own low temperature always about with him; he iced his office in the dogdays; and didn't thaw it one degree at Christmas.*

Nonfiction Example:

In *Obsessive Genius: The Inner World of Marie Curie*, historian Barbara Goldsmith begins the story with what she presumably thought most interesting about her subject, the psychological atmosphere in which Marie grew up.

Marya Slodowski was born in 1867 Poland to very uptight parents, both of whom were schoolteachers. A critical man, her father constantly pushed his five children — one boy and four girls — to excel in academics, which they did.

Yet while developing their children's minds, the parents apparently spent little time nurturing emotional awareness. As a result, Marie never formed an ability to understand what she was feeling, much less verbalize it, which struck me as Marie's defining detail. That emotional blindness, compounded by bouts of terrible depression, motivated Marie to avoid all inner turmoil, which she did by developing an obsessive work habit that helps explain how a two-time Nobel Prize-winning scientist could turn out such spectacular results despite being a mother and a female in a harshly male field.

The One-sentence Test

Although you've had to process an enormous amount of information, don't lose sight of what you need to do: choose the seed from which your character will grow. After doing so, open your *Character* worksheet and under the heading of "Defining Detail" employ the following one-sentence test:

My character is defined by _____.

Again, if the answer doesn't come easily, or if it turns into a paragraph, continue digging until you find one specific detail.

Character Study 4

Our character's defining detail can be found within a childhood incident.

Imagine a 5-year-old little girl in faded yellow flower underpants running down her neighborhood sidewalk, crying. A dry, brown-grass August afternoon, the sky is white, the overhanging trees a deep, dull green as the cicadas pulse. But the girl sees and hears nothing but the roar of an old station wagon as it speeds away from her.

The girl's toes catch on a broken section of concrete and she falls sideways, flips over and sprawls on a lawn being showered by a sprinkler. Blinking water from her eyes, the girl catches sight of the car just as it screeches around a corner and disappears.

The girl wails. Though young, she somehow knows she'll never see her mother again. So abandoned, she develops a deep fear of abandonment that motivates her to avoid further rejection.

Your Character

Exercise 4: Your Character's Defining Detail

Ideally, you'll choose the strategy that appeals to you most and with a little effort, unearth your character's seed. Unfortunately, you may dig in one spot, come up short, and have to dig elsewhere.

Rather than get frustrated, adopt the attitude of a master botanist roaming an unexplored forest filled with wonder and possibility. Have a great time discovering what makes your character unique. Start by reviewing your character's information. Then open your *Self-conversation* worksheet and under an appropriate heading such as "Defining Detail," choose one strategy and begin digging for your character's defining detail. If that doesn't yield the right seed, move on to the next. For example:

Self-conversations

Defining Detail: The most obvious strategy is to define my character via an object since he's such an over-ambitious, materialistic guy. He reminds me of Charles Kane in *Citizen Kane*, the rich but miserable recluse who, on his deathbed, remembers his beloved childhood sled, Rosebud. It's a symbol of everything he no longer has; simplicity, innocence, few worldly possessions, happiness.

What object could explain where my character started in life? A favorite gym shirt from elementary school days? But that's kind of boring and something that could be easily forgotten and thrown out. What about a photo of somebody, like his mother or best friend? But that seems too sentimental. Considering the fortune he eventually accrues, maybe the object could be a reminder of one of his early business ventures, like his first lemonade stand. That's it! Maybe his mother bought the first cup and handed him a shiny new dime he still keeps in his wallet as a talisman.

Now open your *One-sentence Test* document and check the solidity of your thinking, as such:

One-sentence Test

Defining Detail: My character is defined by the first dime he ever earned, a coin he still carries in his wallet as a symbol of his humble, happy beginnings.

When you unearth the right seed from which your character will grow, you'll feel like you've just discovered a completely new type of plant so beautiful, so outrageous it's going to rock the world. Triumphant, it's time to go home and plant the treasure in the hole you've prepared.

Then oh, how your character will grow.

Chapter 5
Letting the Seed Sprout

Watching your character take root is a captivating process. Yet rather than simply observe, you need to understand what you're witnessing so you can direct your character's growth.

We already know a character's defining detail points directly to his motivation, which is rooted in combinations of need, want and fear. Now it's time to discuss how, specifically, a well-defined motivation can help your character grow.

The Benefits of a Well-Defined Motivation

Motivation is integral to our survival because without it, there would be no reason to act. We would be hungry, but not enough to search for food. We would feel pain, but not enough to stop the source of the pain.

What motivation gives us, then, is an incentive to act and so change our situation.

Change
Motivation > action/change

Cells divide, wind shifts, trees are planted and cut down. To live is to change, which is exactly what our storytelling heritage confirms. We fall into and out of love. We fight for our lives, our countries and our souls. We make mistakes, climb unattainable heights and discover the miraculous. We don't just sit around, *we do*.

That's why when we read a story, we *want something to happen*, by which we mean we want the following:

— To see the character take action to change her situation.

— To understand the severity of that action.

— To witness the impact of the action.

If we demand these as readers, we must address them as writers. Doing so will stimulate our character's growth in the areas of admiration, fear and conflict.

Admiration
Motivation > action/change > admiration

Our characters should take action because it's boring and frustrating to read about people who don't do anything. Maybe that reaction has something to do with the survival of the fittest theory; that the more adaptable we are, the greater our chances of survival as top banana on the food chain. After all, we reward those who keep our species advancing — consider Nobel Prize recipients and Olympic athletes — and punish those judged to be dead weight.

Yet doers don't necessarily have to win the grand prize. They need only exert enough effort to change their circumstances, for instance:

— A man who overcomes his debilitating shyness to claim his love for another.

— A destitute woman who starts a business with a $50 loan.

— A journalist who risks his life to uncover a government plot.

Now imagine if they never do anything:

— The man never reaches out for love and so lives a miserable, lonely life.

— The woman never tries to better her situation.

— The journalist is too cowed or lazy to pursue a hot lead.

Do we want to read about such people? No, because even if we hate what some people do — artists who create disturbing pieces, protesters who cause massive traffic jams — we still admire their courage to act, knowing it takes guts to step off secure ground and open themselves to failure.

Think of DeShawn. As soon as she borrows the $50 to start her clothing design business, she makes herself vulnerable in four ways: she forces herself to recognize her greatest weakness; imposes restrictions on herself; uses her greatest talent/exceptional quality; and faces her biggest fear.

Greatest weakness: By taking action, DeShawn must face her personal limitations, which will knock her confidence and heighten her chance of failure. She won't necessarily realize what's often true, that a person's greatest weakness is also her greatest strength. All she knows is that she's too detail-oriented to work quickly, which may sink her business before it's started. Yet that attribute is what allows her to create unique, high-quality clothes that eventually garner acclaim and command a high price.

Self-imposed restrictions: The more actions DeShawn takes, the more she finds it necessary to impose restrictions on herself, which will increase her stress. She sleeps less, works more and spends little time with her 13-year-old daughter, who takes the opportunity to get into trouble. DeShawn also faces a deadline for repayment of the loan.

Exceptional gift/talent: The more pressure on DeShawn, the more she'll use every advantage she's got, which will force her exceptional gift or talent into the open. Realizing she can't work quickly enough, DeShawn will unconsciously rely on her ability to concentrate on one task, no matter the surrounding chaos.

Greatest fear: Defined by a fear of lifelong poverty, DeShawn is motivated to break free. Yet every action she takes will lead her toward what she fears most, a phenomenon we'll soon talk more about.

Nonfiction Example:

In 1972, a charter plane carrying a Uruguayan rugby team crashed in the Andes. The story of the survivors struggle to exist in the harsh mountain environment is recounted in *Alive: The Story of the Andes Survivors* by Piers Paul Read.

Survival stories usually have one thing in common: at least one character who possesses an exceptional will to survive. In the Andes story, that character is 22-year-old Fernando Parrado.

Before the crash, Parrado is an awkward, near-sighted, unimpressive young man. After the crash, Parrado's greatest strength emerges, a fierce determination to escape the mountains, which is also his greatest weakness since he's willing to head off into the mountains unprepared and would do so if not for others. As his desperation increases, his exceptional talent emerges, an incredible gift for cajoling, inspiring and haranguing others into action.

Highly motivated to get out of the mountains, Parrado takes action immediately, even though it means facing his greatest fear, that he'll never escape. Within days of the crash he suggests the two most drastic measures the group eventually takes to survive, that they find a way out of the Andes instead of waiting to be rescued, and eat those who died in the crash.

Is Parrado content to simply make the suggestions? No. He eats the human flesh to gain strength and when ready, attempts to find a way out of the Andes.

Is Parrado an admirable character? Without question.

Fiction Example:

In *Plainsong*, a quiet novel set in rural Colorado, author Kent Haruf creates two old brothers who work the ranch on which they were born. Having never married, these men tend their cattle, repair their equipment and rarely partake of entertainment other than reading farm catalogs and watching TV.

What seems to define these men is an old-school, black and white integrity, where something is either right or wrong and don't bother trying to argue an in between. Their motivation, then, is to be content with what they have and live a life of integrity, even if that means accepting loneliness, love never realized and children never born.

Then one day a teacher in the nearby town drives out and asks if the brothers can take in one of her students, a pregnant teenager. At first stunned, the brothers consider the idea. Not only would it be a big commitment, but having a pretty young girl live with them — two unmarried men — might cause nasty talk in town. Or the girl could accuse them of improper behavior or somehow hurt herself and sue them. Or worse, the brothers could grow to love her like a daughter and she could simply leave.

Yet the brothers accept the risk, seeing this as a chance to experience a life they somehow missed. They clean their home, wash up and wait for the girl to arrive.

Does the act of saying yes to change make them admirable? In the McPheron brothers' words, *I reckon so.*

Fear
Motivation > action/change > admiration > fear

If motivation represents what characters are running to, then it also points to what they're running from.

Consider DeShawn. By taking action to improve her socioeconomic status, she's running from what she fears most: lifelong poverty. What about the man motivated to overcome his shyness and declare his love? He's running from a fear that he'll never love or be loved. And the journalist who risks his life to uncover a plot? He fears he no longer has the guts, brains or stamina to do his job. And Marco? If he's hell-bent to succeed, it's because he's terrified of failure.

When we finally understand our character's greatest fear, our goal is clear: to make him face that fear.

Fiction Example:

Chuck Palahniuk didn't pull any punches when he wrote *Fight Club*. The nameless protagonist hates his job, American consumerism and the sorry, sissified state of maledom. His real problem, however, is that he hates himself.

Motivated to destroy himself, the narrator forms a twisted bond with Tyler Durden, a muscled *man's man* who starts a no-punches-pulled fight club for men, organizes terrorist activities to shake up society and of course, gets the girl.

Tyler pursues his goal of erasing the narrator's personality, but the narrator realizes he can't let that happen because someone has to keep demented Tyler in check. With every action the narrator takes, he comes closer to what he fears most, himself.

Nonfiction Example:

All the President's Men is the famous story by and about the two Washington Post reporters who broke the Watergate scandal surrounding Richard Nixon in the early 1970s.

The authors begin by giving brief, telling descriptions of their defining characteristics via their office reputations: Carl Bernstein's "ability to push his way into a good story and get his byline on it," while Bob Woodward is, "a prima donna who played heavily at office politics." The former a shaggy-haired college dropout who started as a copy boy at age 16, the latter a privileged, clean-cut Yale grad.

Despite their initial dislike for one another, the two seem to share the same defining detail, an extraordinary tenacity that stems from intense ambition and curiosity. Motivated to push the limits, they pool their information, roust interviewees out of bed and take spy-like precautionary measures to meet secret sources. Despite suspicions their apartments are being bugged and those fingered will seek revenge, the reporters continue to act, which makes them highly admirable.

If they're motivated to learn the truth, what are they running from? That they'll never know the truth; that the story will be killed by those in power, or worse, by Woodward and Bernstein through careless errors that end the investigation and discredit them and their newspaper. Instead of backing off, the men push on to face that fear.

Conflict
Motivation > action/change > admiration > fear > conflict

A conflict is a clash between two opposing forces. A character on one side, her worst fear on the other; conflict is what happens when they meet.

If she fears snakes, what will happen if she's forced to work as a snake-handler? If DeShawn fears lifelong poverty, what will happen if a lawsuit threatens to force her into bankruptcy?

Conflicts can be small or large, affect one person or many and have either slight or significant ramifications. A conflict's size and severity is determined by the size and severity of the action leading to the conflict.

Imagine a man arriving at a crowded beach. Seeing a small spot, he politely asks a woman to move a little so he can put down his towel. Because the action is small (a reasonable request) and the severity low (he asks politely), the action has little momentum and only moves the story along slightly.

Now imagine the beach is sparsely populated. The man stomps toward the seated woman, bends over her and says, "Get the hell off my spot!" Much bigger in size and intensity, the action carries enough momentum to propel the story forward.

This example demonstrates what moves stories along: The action of one character forces an equal and opposite reaction in others.

When the man makes a polite request, the woman responds in an equally polite way. When the man yells threateningly, the woman acts as if seriously threatened.

So when thinking of your character's motivation and the actions he'll take, ask yourself the following:

What momentum does the action have based on its size and intensity?

Given the momentum, what impact does the action have on others?

Does the action propel the character toward his fear and so result in conflict?

The last question is usually the most challenging because if the answer is no, we should cut the action, which is often hard to do, especially if it's cool. Yet if the action doesn't lead directly to the character's fear, it's gratuitous and will leave readers wondering, *What does this have to do with anything?*

Remember, too, that actions don't have to be unusual, large, or even visible to have dire consequences. Consider a man who rushes into a crowded elevator. On the way down, he coughs a few times. Of small size and intensity, the coughing seems no more than an annoyance to those around him. Yet what if the man is a scientist who's infected with a deadly, contagious virus he's been working with? The action becomes a bullet: small in size but traveling at high velocity for maximum impact. By running from his fear — that if he gets infected, he won't be able to admit it until it's too late — he runs right into it. And so conflict is born.

Fiction Example:

A team of Jewish boys in 1940s Brooklyn is up to bat against a team of rigidly orthodox Hasids in the opening scene of Chaim Potok's *The Chosen.*

Reuven at bat and orthodox pitcher Danny Saunders on the mound, the baseball is between them, an object of modest mass, though capable of extreme velocity. Danny throws the ball.

Suddenly Reuven is on the ground, hands to his face, the world dark. He feels a sharp, jagged pain in his eye from a piece of his broken glasses. Reuven is in the hospital for weeks, terrified he'll lose his eye. Carrying serious momentum, Danny's action on the field leads to serious impact, which leads to serious conflict.

Nonfiction Example:

In Frank McCourt's memoir *Angela's Ashes*, he tells how his family is so poor and unlucky that after coming to the U.S., they have to go back to Ireland, the ultimate humiliation, given America's reputation as the land of opportunity.

Through it all — an alcoholic father, the death of several siblings, dingy rented rooms next to noxious public toilets — his mother, Angela, finds a way to keep her family barely fed and clothed, for which McCourt admires her deeply. This is a woman who cheerfully refers to her falling-down home as "Italy" and invites in destitute women and children for a cup of tea and a chance to sleep indoors.

If McCourt is a product of street-level survival, then he's motivated to survive at all costs. The symbol of that survival is Angela, a fighter who gives McCourt hope that life won't always be such a struggle. Imagine, then, how McCourt feels when he realizes his mother has to prostitute herself to a despicable slob of a cousin named Laman Griffin just to keep a roof over her kids' heads. Watching his sad mother ascend the ladder to Griffin's bedroom, it's like seeing hope disappear. Facing his worst fear — that he may never rise in life, but rather be sunk by it — McCourt is thrown into deep conflict:

> *She calls up the lane after me, You should have something in your stomach, but I give her my back and turn the corner without answering. I still want to tell her I'm sorry, but if I do I'll want to tell her she's the cause of it all, that she should not have climbed to the loft that night....*

Angela now a symbol of what could happen to him, McCourt acts. He scrapes together enough money to return to America.

Your Role As Author

As the author, you must know your character's motivation so you'll know how he'll act, how others will react and what conflict results.

Your character, on the other hand, may be clueless about what motivates him. Maybe he's a person who acts first and thinks later, like a guy who walks out of his office one day, never to return. Or maybe he plans the action without fully understanding it. Or he may think he knows the reason behind his action, when he doesn't really. Then again, your character may know exactly what he's doing and why.

The One-sentence Test

Now that you fully understand the importance of motivation, it's time to answer the following question in one short sentence:

My character is motivated by . . .

Record the answer on your character's worksheet, which should now include the following items: the character's type, general purpose, specific purpose, defining detail and motivation, including admiration, fear and conflict.

Progress From This Point Forward

Considering that all future growth occurs from this point forward, avoid making major changes that might require you to start over.

While switching a character's defining detail or type qualify as major changes, they can also be subtle. Changing a character's age or ethnicity, for example, can skew his motivation, which would significantly alter his actions and how others react to him. If your protagonist begins as a middle-aged man and you decide to make him a young man, it will affect how he behaves around the young woman support character, and vice versa. The same is true regarding ethnicity and culture. An American girl's belief system might be very different than that of a Saudi Arabian girl. By changing the character from one culture and ethnicity to another, her interior may no longer match her exterior.

That said, it's sometimes necessary to significantly change a character. If so, do it now, not later. And when you do, do it right. Take time to re-seed the character — choose a new defining detail, determine her new motivation, etc. — and let her grow according to her nature instead of simply grafting on significant features that could leave readers wondering, *If it's got the trunk of an apple tree, why is it growing oranges?*

Character Study 5

If our protagonist is defined by a fear of abandonment, she's motivated to avoid further abandonment, a disposition conveyed by the anxious way she looks around, always watching for signs of rejection. She's probably also vehement in believing parents should never abandon their children, no matter what.

Now we can start a self-conversation to help us gauge her attitudes and future behavior:

How hard does she drive herself professionally?

Very. She would never allow herself to be passed over for promotion. That and she's out to please, perhaps feeling if she'd been a better kid her mother would not have left.

How does our character behave in relationships?

She's either hesitant to start them for fear of rejection, or she jumps in too fast and stays too long, unable to admit failure.

Will she ever be the life of the party?

Probably not, considering her underlying anxiety.

Does she surround herself with friends?

Maybe, though it doesn't alleviate her loneliness.

Is she funny?

Possibly, though in a self-deprecating way that covers her sorrows.

What's her greatest strength?

Considering how closely she watches for signs of rejection, she's an excellent observer who often sees more than most about people and situations, a quality that makes her very admirable. At the same time, hyper-awareness is also her greatest weakness because it leaves her open to over-analysis and self-doubt.

If she fears abandonment, what could we do to make her face that fear?

Abandon her.

Agreed. But how?

Let's put her in a small plane over the Australian outback. The plane crashes. She's one of five survivors, the others including two severely wounded businessmen and a mother and her 10-year-old daughter. A small, decrepit plane with a broken radio happens by, the aboriginal pilot saying he only has enough room for four people.

Four people, which means one must stay behind and wait for help. Would our protagonist really deny the two wounded men a chance for medical attention?

No.

Would she split up the mother and daughter?

Absolutely not.

That means our character must accept being left behind for what she thinks will be a day or two.

When two days pass, then three, then five, she knows something bad happened and no one is coming for her. She's left with nothing but a small amount of supplies, her motivation and her exceptional observation skills to save her.

Your Character

Exercise 5: Getting to Know Your Character

It's time to interact with your character in order to discover what makes him admirable, what he fears, how he'll behave and what action will throw him into conflict.

Open your character's *Self-conversations* worksheet and add an appropriate heading such as "Getting to Know My Character." Then drop him into two of the following scenarios and write about how he deals with them. When done, choose three possible scenarios from your own story and do the same.

How does he act in the situation? What does he say? How do other people respond? What expertise or beliefs does he draw on to cope? If he fails, how does it happen and what effect does it have on him? Write as long as necessary to get a feel for how your character talks, acts and reacts, whether a paragraph or several pages. The goal is to understand him so intimately that if a friend says, "Well how would he act if __ happened?" you'll know.

Exercise Scenarios

Choose two scenarios from this list and three from your own story. Again, the question is, what would your character do if dropped into:

— a rugged monthlong wilderness adventure in Alaska

— a crowded, upscale Manhattan restaurant

— a southwestern Native American reservation

— a Las Vegas convention for psychics

— a guerilla war in South America

— a university's anatomy dissection lab

As you watch your character grow, don't be surprised to feel an increasing fondness of and protectiveness toward her. You should also feel a sense of expansion as your imagination opens and you begin to see the possibilities of what your character can do and become, a feeling that will only increase as you lean your head back and watch your character race skyward.

Part III: Growth, Cultivation, Care

Pruning doesn't hurt a healthy plant; rather, it stimulates new growth and enhances the plant's vigor, beauty, and disease resistance. And that's not all. Pruning can improve a plant's appearance, correct or repair damage, direct growth, improve health, rejuvenate, control size, and increase production of flowers and fruits.

— *Smith & Hawken: The Book of Outdoor Gardening*, edited by Smith & Hawken, Workman Publishing

Chapter 6
Freedom to Grow

Why Characters Need It

Where there was once nothing but a patch of dirt, you dug a hole and planted a character's potential. The moment that character put down roots and began to grow, she assumed an active life of her own. Now it's your job to help her succeed. The first step is to allow her to live, *truly live*, by allowing her the freedom to grow according to her nature. In other words, treat her as a real person.

And what do we know about real people? They possess free will. They make decisions that can be influenced by others, but can never be guaranteed. Even when we exert extreme power over people, there's no certainty they'll do as we command. Free will is what makes people unpredictable, and in turn, interesting, exciting and alive. If we want our characters to exhibit these attributes, we should allow them to possess free will, too.

Free will is also what drives great stories. When characters are allowed to act according to their natures, they instigate a chain of believable actions that lead to believable conflict, a process known as plot.

How Freedom Affects Plot

Plot is the chain of events that tells a story. The plot of *King Kong* consists of a chain of events that lead to a giant gorilla climbing the Empire State building. The plot of Alice Walker's *The Color Purple* involves a chain of events that lead to the inner independence of a brutally abused poor black woman.

King Kong could be described as plot-driven, whereas *The Color Purple* could be categorized as character-driven. But such popular catchphrases are highly misleading. Plot-driven, for example, implies the story's action is more important than the characters, which upon closer inspection is not at all true. Action stories featuring terrific characters sell well, whereas stories with unbelievable, one-dimensional characters languish no matter how many car crashes and explosions occur.

Consider King Kong. An imprisoned beast who does his valiant best to free himself, ultimately sacrificing his life for the welfare of the beautiful and compassionate Ann Darrow, King Kong is a great character. Defined by his anger at being unjustly captured, he's highly motivated to escape and highly admirable for his strength and perseverance. His every action brings him closer to what he fears most, death, the ultimate loss of freedom. If he weren't such a great character, the story would never have survived the test of time.

When people say they like plot-driven stories, they're not saying they're willing to swallow cliché characters for the sake of showy action. What they really want are great characters who choose big physical actions that are highly dramatic and have a grave impact on a lot of people, like risking their lives to rescue others. They're usually featured in genre fiction such as thrillers, science fiction, westerns and mysteries, and action nonfiction stories of true crime or high adventure.

The term character-driven implies the story's characters are more important than the plot. But remember that we said admirable characters are doers who take action. The trick is there are two types of action. External actions are visible to others and usually physical, whereas internal actions are often invisible and emotional, such as when a man realizes he's in love. When people say they like character-driven stories, they're saying the characters' actions don't have to be predominantly external, but rather can be largely internal.

Such characters are typically featured in romance stories and literary fiction as well as literary nonfiction involving people whose mental, emotional and spiritual abilities exceed their physical prowess.

So instead of planting your characters in holes that don't quite fit and tempt readers to bypass your work for being *just plot-driven trash* or just *character-driven drivel*, throw out those old, misleading phrases and think of your characters as driven by free will. When you give your characters the freedom to choose those actions — whether external, internal or both — that stem from their natures and defining details, your story will be more than a vehicle for just plot or just character. It will feature both and come alive through characters who resemble people like us, people who instinctively choose external and internal actions appropriate to their natures.

Even adventure lovers think about what they read, ponder their relationships and undergo deep emotional changes. The same is true for those who prefer rigorous cogitation to physical risk-taking. While they probably don't ski black diamond slopes, they may be black belts in karate or entertain people with their boisterous arguments, aggressive mannerisms and silly humor.

So above all else allow your character the freedom to grow according to her nature rather than your expectations. Instead of demanding she act in a certain way, allow her to surprise you by reacting in ways you hadn't anticipated. Let her lead you where she needs to go and learn what she needs to learn.

The Results of Censorship

Under optimal circumstances, writers would be like scientists who plant experimental seeds and observe the resulting growth with a mixture of 99 percent curiosity and one percent expectation. But most of us do the opposite. We bury new growth under the weight of our expectations, then sit back and wait for those expectations to be gratified. We do this with our kids, careers, love lives and friendships.

What happens, though, when a situation is not completely under our control, which is usually any time we deal with other people? The situation turns in a completely different direction. Those of us who like change adapt quickly. We drop our expectations, admit our ignorance of the future, adopt a willingness to learn, let our curiosity take over and allow our character to take the lead.

The rest of us typically view change as a loss of control and a threat to our authority and so tighten our grip. We attempt to regain that control and authority by forcing the character to grow according to our expectations rather than his defining detail. We're particularly vulnerable to this reaction when dealing with protagonists, characters who don't share our values, or when thinking about how to market our work.

Protagonists: We tend to exert the most control over our protagonist because our entire story revolves around him. If he doesn't do as we say, we can't tell our story. This *fit-the-character-to-the-story* attitude grows even stronger when we have a particular ending in mind. Yet if we order our protagonist to do things he normally wouldn't, readers will detect his status as chief puppet and stop reading.

Differing values: We're particularly vulnerable to forcing our opinions on characters whose values conflict with our own. For example, say we're writing a contemporary young adult novel about a middle school juvenile delinquent who's got a serious problem with anger and authority and tries to shock adults with bad language. Every third word out of his mouth is a vile curse word, right?

To which we might say, *Wrong!*, because we personally object to swearing and believe our readers should not be exposed to such a thing. Therefore, we clean up our character's language so that he says, "And don't come near me again!" when what he'd really like to say is, "You come near me again you bitch, you motherfucking asshole, and I'll rip your fucking heart in two!"

Which response rings truer considering the nature we've assigned him?

Marketing our work: But what if we feel pressured to control our character's actions and language in order to find a publisher or keep an audience?

Writing with a specific market in mind has definite advantages. You have a much better chance of getting published if you know exactly what a publisher or audience wants. Also, companies that publish well-established series in particular genres have very clear guidelines to follow in terms of length, language and plot development, which makes writing easier if you don't mind a formulaic structure. And if you manage to break into a market, there's certainly nothing wrong with writing more of the same in order to make a name for yourself while earning money.

In contrast, writing what you want and then finding a market is a more arduous process, especially if your work doesn't fall into a category that can be easily marketed.

Given the realities of today's publishing world, is it really so bad to limit your character's growth just a little in order to get published?

Ultimately the decision lies with you. But remember that it's difficult to create great characters when you restrict their behavior to fit a certain market, meet a moral standard or adhere to a particular plot. If any of these occur, it would be better to face your character, admit your irreconcilable differences and part company rather than enslave your character to your desires, since doing so almost always stunts a character's growth and leads to author insertion, both of which result in loss of believability.

Stunted Growth

Picture a bush that when planted in the proper climate grows into an enormous, lush mass of slender, silver limbs and gorgeous hot pink blooms.

Now picture that bush by the front door of a suburban house, far from its native land and severely trimmed to a 3-by-3 box that's all woody twigs and no blooms. Its girth is further restricted by wire while a stake runs through its middle, all in an attempt to make it grow according to the homeowner's expectations. A beautiful sight? Hardly.

But that's exactly what can happen if we make our character act according to our wishes rather than her defining detail.

Imagine a teen girl, contrary to the core, who hates being told she's just going through a phase. A tall, husky girl who simmers with hilarity, she loves to confound people and so is compliant when she should rebel and rebellious when she should comply.

Now imagine a boy who, in front of a large crowd they both know, dares her to have sex with him. While any other girl would tell him to take a flying leap, this girl says, "Sure," as if accepting a ride home. We're horrified. We think, *But I'm against teen sex,* or, *The publisher won't go for it,* or, *Parents won't allow their kids to read this story.* So instead of following her lead, which may or may not lead to sex, we seize control, have her suffer the stereotypical spasm of doubt and allow her to back out. In one slash we've hacked a prize winning rose bush to the ground just as its flowers began to bloom.

Author Insertion

Author insertion occurs when authors allow their opinions or intent to shine through the narrative when it shouldn't. It originates from *moral objections/natural bias* or a *desire to preach*.

Moral objections/natural bias: Let's return to the model of a troubled youth. We're told the youth is a bad egg and given a history of his misdeeds, yet when he speaks, he sounds like he'd be laughed out of juvenile hall for his clean, spineless, out-of-date language. He puzzles us further by changing his attitude fairly quickly due to a sincere mentor, a last chance or an event that serves as a wake-up call.

How does this character's mild language and quick, dramatic turnaround jive with his actions? It doesn't. Rather, it leaves us scratching our heads and looking to real life for guidance. Does this boy act like the emotionally troubled people we've met? No. Those with serious problems usually behave badly and rarely turn their lives around quickly, if at all.

How are we to interpret the fact that this boy's actions don't match his defining detail or our reality? The only way we can, by surmising that the author had a specific, inflexible intent when writing the story. She needed the character to end up in a particular spot and made him do what was necessary to get there, even though it meant forcing him to act in a way contrary to his original design. Whenever I see this occur, I think of Cinderella's ugly stepsister trying to squeeze her big foot into the dainty glass slipper while insisting, "It fits!"

A desire to preach: A second form of author insertion occurs when writers use a character as a vehicle for preaching, which we'll define in the broadest sense as *a strong personal opinion about what others should do regarding a particular matter*, as opposed to providing others with information and allowing them to make their own choice.

There's nothing wrong with strong opinions as long as we're up front with our readers. That means explaining what we'll be preaching about, whether it's religion, politics, parenting or other beliefs. For example, when writing nonfiction, we could open with, "In this book, I'm going to provide 101 excellent reasons why you should become a vegetarian," then allow readers to decide if they want to listen to our message.

In fiction, there are four perfectly legitimate ways to preach. We can

— identify ourselves as an opinionated narrator. For example, "I'm usually a likable person, except when it comes to cheating spouses. The way I see it, the big 'I,' as I call it, is the cheapest, most low-down sin there is."

— label the story a fable, which immediately alerts readers that the purpose is to impart a moral lesson, the classic identifier being, "Once upon a time…."

— submit our sermons to publishers who agree with our viewpoint and market to audiences that expect our message.

— deliver the sermon through a character so long as the preaching is consistent with her defining detail.

When we clearly state our intent, we give our readers a choice about whether or not to continue reading. If we slip a sermon into our story, either accidentally or otherwise, we take away that choice.

Admittedly, some of us don't realize we're preaching and simply get overwhelmed by our passion for the subject. For example, say an author is writing a biography of his mother and writes the following scene about one of the family's many Thanksgiving dinners:

Mom would make us stay in the living room until exactly 3:30 p.m., just as the light began fading from the winter sky. Then dressed in he full-length gown of watered green silk and wearing a leaf-shaped diamond brooch over her heart, she would invite us in. Her eyes scrutinizing our attire for the right mix of respect and formality, we would enter the dining room as though first-time guests in Wonderland, the room transformed into a spectacular display of color and scent. A centerpiece of deep green evergreen fronds, a cut glass bowl of cranberry and orange relish and the 50-year-old long-stemmed wine glasses graced the table, all as steam curled from the gravy bowl and candlelight glinted off wedding silver. Like many American families, we ate turkey every year, a habit I broke after realizing how inhumanely turkeys are treated on large farms. I went on to research other forms of animal rearing for consumption....

By sermonizing, the author takes the spotlight off the story's main character and places it on himself, thus changing the story from a biography to an autobiography.

To avoid this trap of unintentional preaching, ask yourself the following question at every stage of storytelling: *Is this action consistent with my character's defining detail and lead him to face his worst fear?* If not, excise your sermon and make it into an article for a market open to your viewpoint. Or you can change the story's format to one that accommodates your preaching.

Now let's address those of us who have a burning desire to get our message out, yet understand we might lose readers through direct sermonizing. So we consider ambush tactics, like hiding behind our characters until we can jump out with our message. Or we remain behind our character and hope readers don't notice the preaching. Or we slip our viewpoint in here and there, hoping to indirectly influence our readers.

While ambush tactics are tempting, here are four excellent reasons to resist them:

Us: If we're proud of our message we should speak openly about it.

Our readers: If readers suspect they're being manipulated, they'll feel angry and betrayed, and rightfully so. They set out on our journey in good faith and we led them to expect one thing and then gave them another, just like poor Ralphie in Jean Shepherd's novel and subsequent screenplay, *A Christmas Story*. A young boy in 1940s America, Ralphie spends months waiting for his Ovaltine Secret Decoder Ring. When the package finally arrives, he rips it open and uses the ring to decipher The Most Secret Message of All Time, which turns out to be *Drink more Ovaltine*.

The story: Subtle proselytizing can overshadow our character's story and annoy and bewilder readers. While they might forgive us a few lapses of judgment, they'll give up if they decide we're more interested in our message than in our character.

The character: If we're attempting to make a character live, the last thing we want is to have our voice come out of her mouth because that breaks the magic and leads readers to assume the character was never really alive, but rather simply a prop behind which we hid.

The Results of Unhindered Growth

If we still hesitate to allow our character his freedom for fear of losing control, here's a final argument to assuage our concern: our character cannot get away because he's tethered to us by his defining detail. Even if he shoots skyward, we'll retain a firm grip on who he is and where he began.

So let the character go. Such freedom will allow him to remain consistent and believable, and as a result, change in an organic way.

Consistency and Believability

A character should be true to himself in both interior belief and exterior action no matter how unsettling or distasteful his behavior becomes.

If he's defined by his fear for humanity and believes it can be saved by blowing up the world, that's what he must attempt.

If she's defined by an intense bravado, let her smile through one disaster after another until her mouth and heart break.

If he's defined by an unshakeable belief in his supreme intelligence, considering he's the smartest kid in second grade, let him attempt to find a cure for his mother's incurable cancer.

In other words, let your character get into trouble, the more the better.

Let the bright, creative mother of the legendary Thanksgiving feasts fall into alcoholism. Allow Marco to experience one failure after another as his hope of glory strains to the point of breaking. Heap embarrassments upon a painfully self-conscious teenage protagonist. In your nonfiction account of a mountain expedition gone wrong, explain every mistake made, every problem encountered, every grueling and demeaning thing the survivors did to survive.

Admittedly, we grow so fond of our characters that it's tough to watch them fail. How can we let them suffer when we're in a position to save them?

The answer is, because we know 1) we'll get our character out of trouble by using his defining detail as a guide, and 2) we know his suffering will lead to his moment of personal change — the bad guy realizes he's sunk, the good guy finally understands what it takes to be happy — which is usually also the story's climax.

Personal Change: the Organic Way

Defining detail > motivation > action/change > admiration > fear > conflict > personal change

Organic means natural rather than artificial. Therefore, an organic change is one that results from a natural progression.

If we plant a seed and water it, the seed will send down roots, sprout and continue to change according to its genetics. Similarly, when we plant a character's defining detail, a motivation takes root and fuels the actions and changes that lead a character to his greatest fear. A crucial stage, the character's growth can go either way. If he fails to confront his fear, his growth will plateau and he'll remain in a state of limbo that will eventually bore or frustrate readers. But if he acknowledges his fear and resolves to defeat it, he'll continue to grow by experiencing a personal change.

Imagine a female warrior who finally, after arduous pursuit, finds the dragon and faces her worst fear: she won't have the guts to avenge her father's death at the hands of this beast. As the dragon nears, she raises her sword and — turns and runs away.

If that happens, our readers will turn and run away, too. After all, they think she's a doer and expect her to do something about her fear, which means taking steps to defeat it.

Her actions should stem directly from her defining detail, a village-imposed tattoo on her wrist that marks her as a coward due to a crime her father committed (a misunderstood deed, to be sure). Motivated to clear her father's good name and throw off the stigma of cowardice, she goes in search of the dragon. Admirable for her exceptional ability with weapons-related magic, her greatest strength is tenacity, which is also her greatest weakness, in that she pushes farther and faster than she should.

Then one fateful day she and the dragon meet. The warrior looks up at the towering figure of fire and bad breath and finally understands what she fears most: cowardice. At the same moment she realizes others placed the label on her. The attribute neither genetic nor deserved, she was born with the same capacity for bravery as anyone else, which means *that dragon is toast.*

By acknowledging her fear and taking action to defeat it, the warrior experiences a profound personal change by seeing herself in an entirely new way.

Now let's turn to Marco. If his defining detail is a moment of glory on the ball field when he was 12 and his greatest fear is that he'll never recapture that glory, what will lead to an organic personal change?

Let's say that after getting into a lot of trouble — he starts a sports betting enterprise, gets involved with the mob, watches his house burn down and his German ex-wife kidnapped — he's chased into a deserted baseball stadium one night. He finds himself backed against a wall near the home team dugout. Before him stands a 6-foot-5 tough guy. If Marco can somehow best this thug, he vows to collect his million bucks and his ex-wife and scram to anonymity in the Caribbean. But how can our hero beat this human bull?

He could give in to the thug, but that would mean giving up his dream of glory, which would hardly be satisfying for us or our readers.
He could strike a deal with the thug. But again, he's after glory and there's little glory in compromise.

Or, being a diehard believer to the end, Marco could surreptitiously feel around for anything with which to defend himself, his fingers finding a bat.

Memories of his moment on the mound 30 years ago flood in as Marco swings with perfect form. This time it's a home run! Having defeated his enemy and his fear, Marco boats off to paradise with his blonde babe.

The One-sentence Test

Even if you don't yet know the details of your character's personal change — how and when it will happen — you should know your character's greatest fear.

Using the one-sentence test, answer the following question:

My character's personal change involves overcoming his fear of _____.

As always, don't move on until the answer is clear.

Nonfiction Example:

Trisha Meili, author of *I Am the Central Park Jogger*, is a terrific example of a character who experiences an organic personal change. The growth is so clear we can easily follow it:

Defining detail: a belief she's not living up to her true potential.

Motivation: to overachieve and so prove her worth.

Action: She excels in school, gets on the fast track at a prestigious firm and runs every night to keep her body in peak physical condition. While running alone, she's attacked and suffers severe head trauma. Again, she pushes herself to recuperate and after months of therapy, rejoins her old firm.

Admirable: for her drive to succeed, this time by reclaiming her previous life.

Fear: that she's somehow not good enough, a feeling exacerbated by her cognitive challenges stemming from the head trauma.

Conflict: to publicly identify herself as the Central Park jogger and so admit she's a damaged person and hence, no longer good enough, or remain in anonymity.

Personal change: Meili takes two actions to overcome her fear. She gives a speech and discloses her identity. Then she gets a neurological evaluation to measure the extent of the damage. Both actions lead Meili to realize that, after so many years of trying to prove otherwise, she is not mentally as capable as she was before the attack, yet it doesn't matter because being Trisha Meili is good enough.

Fiction Example:

Richard Wright gives us a stark depiction of his protagonist's dramatic — and organic — personal change in the novel *Native Son* published in 1940.

Twenty years old and living in the slums of Chicago, Bigger Thomas is a black man who's trying to support his mother and two other siblings.

Defining detail: wants to be a good and honorable man.

Motivation: to survive life with his dignity intact.

Action: gets a respectable job as a chauffeur for a wealthy white family.

Admirable: tries hard to play by the rules of a society separated into white and black.

Fear: ruination; that something will happen to kill his chance of living decently.

Conflict: In an attempt to keep his job, Bigger breaks the rules of white society regarding its prohibition of contact between white females and black men in order to help carry his employers' drunken daughter to her room after her date with another man. When the daughter's blind mother walks in, Bigger is so terrified of being caught he remains quiet while holding a pillow over the daughter's face, accidentally killing her.

Personal change: Bigger strikes out to protect himself in an unfair fight with a society that's cornered him. Faced with ruination, he realizes that like himself, his victims were trapped by circumstance. In turn, we pity Bigger for his inability to see that he's just a speck in a much bigger problem of a society split by racial hatred that's passed from one generation to the next.

Note that Bigger's personal change is not necessarily what we want. Wouldn't it be better if Bigger understood how white society set him up for failure? Wouldn't it be great if he made a dramatic speech on the courthouse steps about how his race is terribly wronged and one day the world will come to see the injustice? What a fantastic Hollywood moment!

But it would also strip Bigger of his believability by producing more from him than his nature dictates. Defined as a poor, uneducated man who's led to believe the white race is superior, readers expect him to act within those boundaries.

Character Study 6

When we last left our character, we decided to drop her into the Australian outback, an event designed to sink her so deeply into conflict she experiences an organic personal change. While she won't reach that point in this chapter, she will start walking toward it, which means thinking about how she'll act and how she might change based on her defining detail, a fear of abandonment.

As we contemplate, we'll ask ourselves, 1) would our character act as such, and 2) will this action lead to the character's personal change? We'll write our thoughts and possible scenarios on our *Self-conversation* worksheet under an appropriate heading such as "Organic Actions/Change." For example:

Organic Actions/Change

Our character could sit in one place for five miserable days until being rescued. But then she wouldn't be a doer. What action would make her a doer? She could study the immediate area to determine if there's any water, food or shelter that could help her survive. Yet while that would help, being rescued after five uncomfortable days would not necessarily be enough to push her face-to-face with her fear.

An Aboriginal man could happen by, lead her to his village and then escort her to where she can get transportation. Their travel together, coupled with his wisdom, could be interesting. But that still leaves the two problems: the situation wouldn't be traumatic enough to force an inner crisis and if the Aborigine becomes the doer, our character would lapse into the role of follower.

Our character could rescue herself and in the process forgive her mother. While this scenario holds the most promise, it's still too vague to be plausible. Considering she's spent almost her entire life grieving her mother's loss, how could she erase the pain through one experience? Unless, that is, something happens during her journey to radically change her thinking.

Your Character

Exercise 6: The Truth Test

It's time to see if you understand and accept the most important facet of this chapter: your character must grow according to her nature.

On your *Self-conversation* worksheet, create a heading titled "The Truth Test." Beneath that, write something you don't understand about your character; an attitude, action, tendency. Choose something that's potentially controversial for you as well as pertinent to the story. If you're a staunch environmentalist, for example, and your nonfiction character is the opposite, you could write, "I don't understand why this character pollutes without ever feeling guilty." Then proceed to have a direct conversation with the character.

The point of the exercise is twofold: 1) to see if you can allow your character to be her own person, no matter how much it upsets you, and 2) to keep asking why until you understand her viewpoint:

Me: Do you care about the environment?

Character: I don't know. I don't think about it a whole lot.

Me: You're not worried we're messing up the planet?

Character: Not really.

Me: How can you say that?

Character: Because it's true.

Me: Aren't you worried about global warming, rising sea levels and cancer-causing pollutants in the air and groundwater?

Character: Not really. And I heard global warming isn't a proven theory.

Me: How can you possibly say that! Only those who don't know any better would —

Character: Are you calling me ignorant?

Me: (angry retort ready, reminder to calm down, thoughtful pause) I don't understand your position and I'd like to. Let me rephrase my question. Why aren't you worried about the environment?

Character: Well, it's like this. I think we're a skanky species in general. We lie, we cheat, we kill each other and everything around us, concreting over flowers and wiping out endangered owls and stuff. We're our own worst nightmare, except for this one cool fact: we're scrappy as hell. Like a 90-pound nothing managing, at the last possible moment, to ding the dragon between the eyes and avert a horrible death. The environment, wars, every imaginable mess we get ourselves into; we always find a way to wiggle free. I think that's what'll happen with this environment thing. We'll bring ourselves to the point of extinction, then manage to save ourselves.

Note that at first the character seems apathetic and shallow, as if she can't be bothered with thinking about anything weightier than celebrity fashions. Yet we learn she not only thought about the subject, but also developed a fairly optimistic philosophy. While we may not subscribe to her point of view, we understand it and respect the fact she's formed an attitude that helps her survive in this world.

In short, learning to understand and tolerate a character's differences rather than make her see the world as we do is key to creating a great character. Where there's tolerance, there's freedom, and where there's freedom there's growth.

So allow your character the freedom to live life as she sees fit. Only then will her nature take over and allow her to grow to her proper dimensions.

While it may seem she's completely independent of you now and that you're little more than a hanger-on, nothing could be farther from the truth.

Your character still needs you, probably more than you both know.

Chapter 7
Helping Your Character Grow

While most plants grow readily once established, master gardeners know they must direct that growth to encourage the emergence of a plant's true potential. We need to do the same for our character, which is why she still needs us.

Having just talked about how characters need their freedom, it's important to understand the difference between *control* and *direct*. Control means forcing characters to do what we want, whereas direct means helping them make decisions based on their nature. The former an attitude of selfishness, the latter stems from a true desire to see our characters do the best they can.

How to Begin: Extrapolation

Now that you know your character's defining detail, motivation, exceptional quality, strength, weakness and fear, it's time to extrapolate about her background and current situation by using self-conversation to answer such questions as, *What does my character look like? How do others react to her? What's his family history?*

Besides learning more about your character, you'll also begin to compile a list of possible scenes.

More Details

Let's return to our female warrior from the previous chapter. We already know the most important things about her — an ignoble wrist tattoo, a fear of cowardice, an exceptional ability for weapons magic — it would hardly do to repeat those few facts over and over. Instead, we need more details that help readers picture her in their minds while explaining where she's been and where she wants to go.

In terms of physical characteristics, our female warrior is tall with narrow hips, broad shoulders and the pale gray skin and light green eyes of her race. She lives in an isolated room of a cliff-side fortress. Regarding family history, she's the fourth daughter of Aarion, the Peacekeeper of the Third Clan of Dyor. Her extraordinary ability for weapons magic allows her to speed and otherwise alter her movements in order to gain the advantage during any altercation involving weapons. Her favorite weapon is a tinga, or thin chain of magic-enhanced metal she wears like a necklace until the moment she needs it.

A few extra details, yet she's more interesting already.

While we could go on about her favorite foods, how she was educated, the history of her world, etc., we want to avoid slowing down her journey with inessential details. Therefore we need to establish each detail's necessity by asking whether it stems from her defining detail and leads to her personal change. If it doesn't, leave it out.

For example, if we know our character has to fight a dragon, we should include details that make such an event possible. She has to live in a world where dragons exist, have a reason to fight the dragon and be able to reach the monster in a land where people either walk or ride horses, which provides an opportunity to describe her physical prowess, tracking ability and advantage over the dragon. If her favorite flower, the sparkling wool-op, gives her an idea of how to defeat the beast, include it, otherwise cut it.

Possible Scenes

A scene consists of the continuous actions within a specific moment. A young boy sits at a picnic table in the park, smiling, as his mother advances with a birthday cake while friends and relatives clap.

Then we show the boy walking toward a swing. An obvious break in continuous action, as well as change of location, readers understand that a new scene has begun.

A character's action can lead to one or more scenes, depending on the momentum of that action. If the birthday boy asks his mother to go home — a small action with little momentum — it's probably only worth one scene. But if the boy has a seizure — a big action with a lot of momentum — the event probably leads to several scenes in which someone attempts CPR, the boy rides in an ambulance, the parents wait as he undergoes surgery, etc.

Some people prefer to compile a detailed list of scenes from the story's start to finish before writing, while others prefer to begin writing a scene and see where it leads. Either way, extrapolation is an excellent tool for discovering future scenes.

If we know readers expect our female warrior to leave on her quest shortly after the story begins, we can begin with a scene where she's humiliated yet again in front of her entire community. Finally fed up, she decides to leave, though she isn't sure where to go and neither are we. Turning to extrapolation, we decide she finds an obscure book that gives clues about where the dragon lives, which leads to a series of short scenes in which she packs up and leaves. Finally out on the road, there's a scene where she faces the first of her many challenges, and so forth.

Such extrapolation works equally well with nonfiction. If you're writing about a well-known historical figure and have a long list of actual events, you could recount all of them. Yet that might make readers feel as though they're reading an encyclopedia:

Ellen Rosen was born on Aug. 12, 1913, in New Haven, CT. She was the youngest of five children born to Margaret and Harold Rosen. Her father moved them to Farmington when Ellen was 4. A year later, her mother and two older sisters became a victim of the great influenza epidemic of 1918. Ellen went to the local school until age 11....

Extrapolation, on the other hand, allows you to uncover the event that proved most pivotal to her development. If Ellen's defining detail is an intense love for her mother, we can guess her mother's death was crucial to forming our character's interest in science and specifically in what caused her mother's death. Motivation established, we can skim past unnecessary details to those directly related to her ambition. Maybe we show the local teacher advising Ellen's father to enroll her in an accelerated school with a challenging science curriculum. That leads to a scene where Ellen's science teacher becomes her mentor, which leads to Ellen's first day at a competitive all-male East Coast University, etc.

Extrapolation also often reveals the perfect name for fictional characters or helps determine the best way to refer to nonfiction characters, whether formally, such as President William Clinton, or by a nickname such as Bill.

What a Great Name Can Accomplish

While it may seem strange to start talking about names so far into the character's development, consider that choosing a name first and a defining detail second can lead to problems of limitation and cliché.

Limitation: Say you name your character Daisy and, due to the subtle influences of cliché, think of her as ultra feminine, excessively cheerful and somewhat flighty. Yet as you begin her development, you realize she's got to be tougher and not so cheerful; that she seems more like a Dakota than a Daisy.

So why not simply change her name?

Because if you're now thinking of the character differently, she probably is different, which means you'll have to go back and re-seed her with a new defining detail.

Cliché

Choosing a name too soon also means you might pick something boring or cliché. While it's true many of us have mainstream, unexciting names, it's also true that there's more variation than we think. Instead of being mostly Jeffs, Susans, Teds and Lisas, many of us have really distinct names like Dimple, Rock, Rafaela and Solie. If this seems unbelievable, go to your phone book and take a look.

While you're at it, note that the unusual names are rarely cliché vis-à-vis soap opera names, which, if you're tempted to use them, can date your story and make it sound melodramatic.

So instead of trying to squeeze your character into a name you chose, let him lead you to the right name. Until that day arrives, there's nothing wrong with calling him "X."

For You and Your Character

Using a name simply to differentiate one character from another exploits only a small fraction of a name's true value, which if given a chance can convey an enormous amount about your character, from sex, race, ethnicity, religion and economic status to family history, culture, parentage and even physique.

Take the name Bubba. What image does it conjure? A white Christian man (race, sex, religion) from the South (region, culture), he's blue-collar (economic status), of average intelligence (parentage) and beefy stature (physique). He loves car races, TV wrestling and guns (culture). Although a cliché, it gives you an idea of how effectively a name can describe a character without blatantly doing so. The example also serves as a warning about choosing names at random, lest you pick one that conveys the wrong image for your character. If he's an educated, brilliant Inuit man from Alaska, Bubba is clearly a bad choice.

Then again, it might be the right choice. Besides providing information about a character, a name also reflects his nature via the name's meaning, humor value, contrast to the character's personality, portentous symbolism or sound.

The meaning of a name: Use the meaning of a name to reflect a person's nature. If your character craves victory, name her Caelan, which comes from a Gallic word meaning victorious people. If he's a guy who lives to surf, name him Kai, the Hawaiian word for ocean.

Considering Bubba comes from a German word meaning boy, it turns out the name does fit our man from Alaska. A real Peter Pan of snow land, he loves pranks, games, sports and a carefree lifestyle. The youngest of five brothers and sisters, Bubba was born to an Inuit man and German woman who raise sled dogs.

In terms of nonfiction characters, find out what their first and last names mean as well as where they came from and whether they fit the characters' natures. If the name was unintentionally mangled, explain how. If it was purposely changed, explain why. If the character has a nickname, explain who gave it to him.

Humor value. Names have the potential to house a lot of humor. Think of Bubba. It's very funny to imagine someone who's such a direct contrast to the stereotype of his name. Rather than be a hulking, blue-collar good ol' boy of uncouth manners and dress, our Bubba is a short, fast, twinkle-in-the-eye charmer who also happens to be a renegade physics professor at a big university.

Consider the humor value of other names: Sunny for a woman who's consistently morose; Star for a woman who's dull in every respect; or Plato for a skinny weakling, Plato meaning strong shoulders.

Contrast: A name can also reflect attributes such as irony, reality and hope. Think of a man nicknamed Lucky by his war buddies. A seemingly cruel joke, considering Lucky endured two years of torture in a POW camp, the name instead reflects his buddies' enormous admiration for a man who managed to escape. Think, too, of a destitute mother who names her son Prosper, hoping the name will come true.

A portent: Names are a great way to portend a character's future. Take our boy Prosper who, despite being an impoverished kid, lives up to his name by becoming a successful businessman. Or think of an ugly girl named Padma who grows into the meaning of her Hindi name, goddess.

A name's sound: The sound of a name can instantly conjure a character's persona. Consider the name Rad — as in radical and right on — for a funky, young, lanky-bodied, spiky-haired dude. If you want to convey the lithe sensuality of a young woman, name her Saffron, given its seductive "s" and reference to the exotic, aromatic spice.

Name traps: When done naming all the characters in your story, look at them to judge how they sound together. If you've chosen Donna, Don, Dorothy and Devona, the repetition of "D" might make it difficult for readers to keep track of which character is which. The same can happen when using names that rhyme, like Kenny, Denny and Lenny, or when most of the names have the same number of syllables, such as Roxanna, Katrina and Frederick.

Also, avoid assigning fictional characters truly unusual names that belong to people you've heard about or met, especially if those characters are undesirable. While you might think there's no chance your rotten third grade teacher will ever read your story, she might, and as a consequence, assume you meant to humiliate her and sue for defamation.

Lastly, if you make up a strange name in an attempt to circumvent any possible misunderstandings, do a web search on your creation. If the name matches that of any real people, tweak the spelling until it's unquestionably unique.

Where to Find Great Names

The easiest way to find the right name for your character is to look around and listen. Jot down the names of everyone you know while inquiring about the origin of those names and what they mean. Are they named after a family member, a celebrity or an aspiration, such as Serenity? Or is the name based on geography, such that Cocoa is named after Cocoa Beach, FL, where she was conceived?

Besides asking people, look in your local phone book to discover names like Gregorio, Yanik, Laya, Marielita, Ernestine or Van. If your character comes from another region, contact someone who lives there and ask what names she finds via the same method.

You can also consult baby-naming books or web sites, most of which include each name's meaning. This is a particularly fruitful approach when trying to find a name within a certain ethnicity with which you're unfamiliar, and therefore at high risk for choosing something cliché. If you're tempted to name your French character Jacques or Louis, for example, a fast search could yield something better, like Nouel or Troilus.

If unable to find the right name, you can make up something. This method works particularly well when you want to quickly convey a character's nature and physical stature without relying on clichéd names. If your character is a well-fed country lawyer able to run rings around the big city fellas, give him a name that reflects his bodacious, loquacious, wily style: Boscious Wyle.

Fiction Examples:

There are so many fantastic names in humanity's literary experience that it's hard to give just one example, so here are several:

— Cruella DeVil, the evil, fur-coat wearing murderer of innocent Dalmatians from Dodie Smith's 1956 novel, *101 Dalmatians*.

— Huckleberry Finn, the incorrigible, straw hat-wearing country boy in Mark Twain's *The Adventures of Tom Sawyer* and *The Adventures of Huckleberry Finn*.

— Ishmael, the plainspoken narrator in Herman Melville's *Moby Dick*.

— Pippi Longstocking, the crazy-haired, freckle-faced ruffian from Astrid Lindgren's book of the same name.

Nonfiction Examples:

Nonfiction names can be just as fascinating as those in fiction or even more so:

— Kunta Kinte, the African man kidnapped and transported to America on a slave ship in Alex Haley's famous family history, *Roots*.

— Yo-Yo Ma, the world-renowned cellist who is the subject of *My Son, Yo-Yo* as told by Marina Ma and written by Dr. John A. Rallo.

— Gypsy Rose Lee, a.k.a. Louise Hovick, a famous Great Depression-era stripper who had a sharp business savvy and wit to match, as is evident in *Gypsy: A Memoir*.

— William Henry McCarty, also known as Kid Antrim, William H. Bonney, Billy the Kid, the infamous boy gunfighter of Wild West days as described in Robert M. Utley's *Billy the Kid: A Short and Violent Life*.

Character Study 7

Let's use extrapolation to fill out our character. We begin with the following facts: she's a single female in her early thirties; has a habit of darting her eyes from person to person; and works hard — often too hard — to avoid rejection. Now we can start asking questions.

If our character winds up in the Australian outback, how does she get there in the first place and what will equip her to survive, at least for a while?

Given her keen sense of observation, let's make her a scientist and specifically, a hydrogeologist who completed graduate fieldwork in the Kalahari Desert. Her extensive knowledge of rock and subterranean water systems will be a clear advantage in the outback.

Why is she flying over the outback?

Because she's collecting data for the next World Water Forum.

What should we name her?

Let's call her Adrina, which comes from an Italian word meaning "happiness." A stark contrast to her deep unhappiness and upcoming predicament, the name can also suggest Adrina might find happiness one day. Making the name work a little harder, let's say Adrina's mother chose it from a celebrity magazine. A Vietnamese immigrant, she wanted a name that would bring her daughter good fortune. Or at least that's what Adrina's Vietnamese father once claimed, with derision.

Your Character

Exercise 7: Branching Out

Step 1: Open your character's file and add a fifth document titled *Other Significant Details.* Using what you know about her, begin to list the details that will make her more interesting while moving her story along.

While you've grown your character in chronological order so far, it's time to work backward for a while. At the top of your new document, list the action that will bring about the moment of your character's personal epiphany, otherwise known as the *climax.* Rather than lock her into anything too specific yet, keep the action general, such as, "Climax: when my warrior finally faces the dragon." Then add details based on the following questions:

How did she get to this point? (Means of transportation, physical prowess, help she received, how long did the journey last, etc.)

What led to her current mental state? (Family history, key experiences and observations, who and what pushed her along, etc.)

What equips her to deal with the situation? (Expertise, skills, natural abilities, personality, education, past experience, alliances with others, etc.)

This is an enthralling job that requires full use of your imagination, so enjoy it! Sink into your character's world in order to examine her from all angles. When done extrapolating, separate the necessary from the unnecessary details by asking whether each is 1) consistent with the character's defining detail, and 2) moves the character toward the climax and if so, how? If you're unsure, move the detail under a heading titled "Unsure" so you'll have it if you need it later.

Step 2: Create a sixth document titled *Possible Names* and list every name that comes to mind whether you think it's appropriate or not. When done, evaluate each name based on 1) its meaning, 2) humor value, if any, 3) contrast to the character, 4) its portent, if any, and 5) its sound.

If you have a number of appropriate names, choose the one you like best. If you don't have a favorite, use self-conversation to determine the best choice, asking the character directly if necessary.

Use this same document when creating names for other characters. Feel free to steal names from one list or another while comparing the chosen names to see how well they work together.

Step 3: Create a seventh document titled *Possible Scenes*. Now knowing where your character begins and her moment of personal change, think about what actions will take her from one point to the other, each action generating one or more scenes. Consider the female warrior:

— She begins as an outcast.

— She finds an ancient book that gives clues about where the dragon lives and decides to go after him.

— After packing her bags, she stops by the room of her friend, who gives her a tinga.

— Now out on the road, the warrior spots an eagle high overhead, realizes it's following her and determines to find out what it wants.

Work through the story in chronological order to make sure the character's actions take place in logical order. Once your scenes are organized, you can decide whether to tell the story in chronological order — the most common means of storytelling — or move scenes around and tell the story out of sequence, a technique known as a *broken timeline*.

While compiling your list, include the following information for each scene: 1) scene name, 2) time (actual time, day, date), 3) action, and 4) importance. For example:

Scene Name: Female warrior named G'nay leaves her community

Time: 4 a.m., morning after summer solstice festival

Action: She packs her bags and stops by the room of her only friend, who gives her a tinga.

Importance: This is the first step G'nay takes to change her life for the better.

This exercise will demonstrate how rapidly your character is growing. Rather than take a breather, continue pouring in your energy. You'll not only be amazed by how she'll change with the infusion of your effort, but also by how you'll change.

Chapter 8
Growing With Your Character

There's a marked difference between a plant that simply grows and one that thrives, the first only achieving modest growth, while the other reaches its maximum potential.

While gardeners can encourage plants to flourish by planting the right seeds in the proper soils and locations, none of that will help if the plants aren't watered and fertilized.

But how do you nourish a character? By standing over him with a large watering can? Though a humorous image, it's not far off the mark. But rather than pour water, imagine showering your character with the best of you.

Add Yourself

You've considered, planned, overseen and directed. Now it's time to go above and beyond those standard duties by allowing the best part of you to wash over your character, because it's only by soaking up those mineral-rich nutrients that he'll thrive.

Think of adults who care for children. Their duties mostly include keeping the kids safe while seeing to their immediate needs regarding clothing, food, shelter, etc. But is that enough to make children flourish? Most of us would say no, that it's only when adults allow their love to flow that kids begin to flourish.

While it takes time and emotional bravery to help another life bloom, the effort is as necessary to your character's development as any previous step you've taken so far and results in advantages that are just as measurable and concrete.

Authenticity

Think of all you've experienced in life. Even if you don't have an impressive job title or a movie star lifestyle, you've no doubt interacted with thousands of people and have accumulated a mass of memories involving countless emotions and images. By showering your character with these nutrients, you'll authenticate her experiences.

Begin by considering her present situation and extrapolate about how she might feel based on her defining detail. Angry? Confused? Rapturous? Then recall an incident that made you feel the same way. Why did it make you feel that way? What did you notice in that moment? Is it possible your character could make the same observation?

Even if you don't know what it's like to have your spaceship chased by hostile aliens, remember what it felt like to be chased by an enraged driver who thought you cut him off. How did you feel? Terrified? Like you couldn't catch your breath? Did your skin prickle with sweat? Did your throat constrict as you gripped the steering wheel?

Are these fantastic feelings with which to imbue your character? Yes!

Would doing so make your character's reactions truly authentic and exciting to read? Yes!

Could this use of personal experience be applied to nonfiction characters, as well, especially for creative nonfiction like Truman Capote's "nonfiction novel," *In Cold Blood*?

A thousand times yes. So go ahead, search your life for tidbits that can enrich your character.

Deep Appreciation vs. Shallow

Besides authenticity, passing your emotions on to your character will help you achieve a deeper appreciation for both her and her dilemma. Say we're writing about the true story of a teenage girl who gets pregnant in the late 1960s. After being thrown out by her mother, she lives in a commune where she meets a man heavily involved in a radical counterculture organization that turns violent. As we think about what personal experiences could help make her actions and reactions real, we can't help but develop a better understanding of the character and her quandary. Imagine the moment she learns she's pregnant. Guided by her defining detail, we extrapolate that her heart skyrockets with joy and just as quickly plunges into deep horror. Recalling a similar moment, we remember a swimming competition in which we touched the pool wall and burst out of the water, declaring victory, only to realize we came in dead last.

An awful moment of *I can do it!* followed by *What have I done?*, we now empathize with our character, which will help us crush cliché, considering the more emotionally involved we are, the more we'll see our character as an individual rather than as a type. Think of the pregnant girl's mother. It would be easy to depict her as a stereotypical rotten parent and move on. But by imagining ourselves as that mother — a dead-end job, lousy upbringing, bills, arguments, loneliness — we come to see that she's barely surviving. By recalling a personal incident that made us feel this way, we begin to see how this additional problem shoves her under. Panicked and unable to breathe, she fights to free herself to keep from drowning. Now when we step back, we see her in a whole new light. Though not a nice person, we know she's real and deserves compassion.

Maintaining Your Privacy, and Others'

If you're worried that imbuing your character with your experience will reveal more about you than you are comfortable with, here are five concepts to contemplate:

You should never submit what you don't want people to read. If you've written something that pulls from an intimate experience in your life — perhaps a divorce that's still painful to think about — you're not emotionally ready to submit the work for publication. Instead, let the story rest until the idea of a public display is not simply tolerable, but acceptable. If that never happens, forget publication. Just by documenting the experience, you'll preserve emotions that, when they become less painful, can be used to nourish future characters.

Never reveal more about yourself than you want others to know. If you don't want readers to know you flunked out of college, don't submit a story about it. If you don't want them even guessing you flunked, don't write a scene that's so similar and realistic readers will know it's true. If you don't even want to tap into how the experience made you feel — the embarrassment, the frustration — don't write about the incident at all. Nobody can force you to divulge more than you want to or should.

There's no way for readers to separate fact from fiction. Those of us new to writing may feel that when people read our work, they can spot our personal information, despite attempts to camouflage it. Those of us who have been writing for awhile, however, know the reality: there's no way for readers to know what's real, what's made up or what came from research unless we tell them.

If people ask a question that's too personal, you don't have to answer. Instead, you can say that stories are almost always a combination of what writers put into them, what characters discover for themselves and how readers interpret the story. You can also tell readers — with humor and sincerity — to mind their own business.

You never have the right to invade someone else's privacy. If you plan to write about someone's private life, you should be professional, responsible and ethical, especially if, by making the information public, you could harm the person or others. If you even suspect someone's privacy is at stake or that you could be sued for revealing the information, you should proceed in one of four ways:

1. Ask permission to use the private material.

2. If the person does not give permission, stick to well-documented, verifiable facts regarding him.

3. Change, delete or fictionalize details until readers are unable to recognize the person in question.

4. Wait until the person dies before releasing the information. If there's any question about legality, consult an attorney.

Say we write about a still-living uncle and want to include a rumor that he killed someone in a fight over money many years ago. We could approach the uncle, show him what we plan to write and ask his approval. If he says yes — in writing — we're okay. If he doesn't, he could sue us for slander since the event is based on rumor.

But if the murder and Uncle's involvement were well-documented, we don't need his permission so long as we stick to public domain information, like a 1934 newspaper article stating, "Gerard Perkins was brought in for questioning regarding the murder of Owen Sadowsky, 31, of Stumpville, on March 5. The last person to see the victim alive, Perkins was seen leaving Sadowsky's hardware store less than an hour after authorities believe Sadowsky died of stab wounds to the chest."

While it's important to use accurate information, the next step is to consider whether it's ethical, especially if making such facts known will significantly change someone's private life. Imagine what might have happened if Flora Rheta Schreiber had revealed that Sybil, the woman of 16 personalities, was really Shirley Ardell Mason of Lexington, KY. Instead of leading a quiet, serene life as an accomplished artist after a horrifying childhood and disorienting middle age, Mason's privacy would have been shattered by curiosity-seekers.

Now consider Uncle. If he confessed to the murder, served time and still regrets the killing, is writing about the incident worth adding to his torment? We could wait until he dies, but what if doing so upsets his sister, who happens to be our mother? Is the story worth jeopardizing our relationship?

So when deciding whether to include someone's private information in your story, ask yourself the following questions: 1) can you live with the repercussions of revealing the information, and 2) is the revelation necessary? If you answer yes to both, then write the story, otherwise don't.

But what if you're out for revenge and want to reveal someone's secrets, either through a direct attack or an account so thinly fictionalized readers can't help but recognize him? If so tempted, go ahead and write because you've obviously got a serious need to vent. With any luck, you'll work through your anger and reach a much healthier mental state. Then put the writing aside and move on. Granted, it's inviting to cash in on our society's extremely lucrative tell-all book market. Yet writing is about creating something positive that leads to our character's growth and our own. Whereas there's no growth in revenge.

Allow Yourself to Grow

The best reason to emotionally invest yourself in your character is that doing so will help you grow and flourish, too. Besides gaining insight about your own life, you'll also expand how much you know, feel and can tolerate.

Courage

Growing alongside our characters takes courage because it can change the way we view ourselves and those around us and as a result, alter friendships for better or worse. Opening ourselves up also means admitting we're not yet the best we can be, which is hardly an enticing thought.

Yet to grow is to live. Therefore if we live, we should seek to grow.

Personal Insight

By forcing ourselves to take a closer look at everything and everyone around us, we can't help but discover things we never noticed before or reinterpret those we did.

While most insights are positive, such as when we realize we love someone, others can be painful. Imagine how earthshaking it would be to realize that our character's deepest fear is our own, or that our brutal antagonist is actually based on someone we love.

While we could jam such upsets back into their holes and bury them, we would be suffocating an opportunity for personal growth. That and closing off an avenue of thought lessens your character's depth by barring him from where he needs to go. Therefore, if hit with a difficult revelation, relax and take a break. Proceed only when ready to work through the emotions you awakened. You can record the resulting growth in a personal journal, use it indirectly to deepen your character or use it directly by including stark details that make your story resonate with readers. Hopefully somewhere along the way you'll congratulate yourself. By opening up, you've taken action and become a doer, just like your character.

Open-mindedness

When we grow intellectually and emotionally, we can't help but open our minds to new ideas. Like emotions, some ideas are exciting and easy to accept, while others are almost impossible to countenance. Sometimes it's not even the idea we find troublesome, but what the idea unearths about us, such as that we're bigoted when we thought we weren't, or open-minded, when new ideas actually scare us.

Yet if we want to grow characters who are different from us — in background, education, ethnicity, socioeconomic status, politics, etc. — we've got to be open-minded. The first step is to admit that what's true for us may be untrue for others. That and our opinions may be based on emotion rather than fact. Then we should adopt an attitude of curiosity over pride, given it's only when we become more interested in discovery than in appearing right that we actually learn.

Permission to Learn and Feel

Giving yourself permission to learn and feel means pushing yourself to research and contemplate any threatening, taboo subjects your character has to deal with (incest, racism, etc.). Considering these things will help you empathize with your character. But don't be surprised to find yourself crying over her misery or angry about her stupidity. Many famous writers grieve, laugh, love and blubber right alongside their characters.

Character Study 8

It's time to invest ourselves in Adrina in order to make her behavior more authentic while helping us understand her better. To begin, imagine being 5-foot-2 and only 100 pounds so that friends and their parents constantly encourage you to eat more — you're too thin, you look unhealthy — even when you eat plenty. And they go on about your long, thick hair that's a flat, dull black. You should cut it, they say. You should wear it up.

Knowing you're no beauty, you don't date much. Unable to find a balance between the American in-your-face kind of outlook and the Vietnamese caution of your community, you fall into awkward social limbo of sort-of friendships.

You grow up in a rundown San Jose neighborhood of Vietnamese immigrants, just you and your father in a small apartment a block from the interstate. Your dad works in a print shop, you go to school. He sometimes grumbles about your mother, how moody she was, and how lazy. Neither of you talks about the day she left.

Instead you grow up on the malnourished chatter of your dad and neighbors. How's school? Did you buy mint leaves and tea on the way home? How's your father? How are you? To which you learn to say, Fine, I'm fine, always fine. Because you know people don't want to be bothered by people who are not fine; that when you're not fine, they leave. So you keep your mouth closed and try to be cheerful, though it takes increasingly more effort, which drains the strength you need to remain the top student in your school. You keep fighting, even though you feel like you're on the verge of losing a marathon you've been running for years. One slip, one hesitation and you'll be left behind in the world of *not fine.*

Except when you swim. When you swim, you don't do laps. Rather, you plunge in and stay under as long as you can, loving the cool silence, all noise and doubt gone. So that when you reach college, there's no question of what you'll study. Eight years later you're a Ph.D. in hydrogeology with an emphasis in hydrology.

Now when we stand back, we see Adrina in a whole new light. We feel her quiet, unacknowledged suffering and view her determination with reverence, knowing we probably would have crumbled under such persistent inner demons long ago.

As we compile scenes leading Adrina toward her fear, conflict and personal change, we consider how she feels, offer her what we know and when necessary, empathize. When she's in her office until late and a colleague urges her to go home, we urge her, too, but know she won't. We think back to an occasion where we felt compelled to stay, too, and understand her unhappiness and anxiety, which increases when she realizes she's late to meet her newest boyfriend. Arriving at the restaurant, she smiles and shrugs in apologia. To us, the boyfriend seems only mildly annoyed, but our hypersensitive, sharp-eyed, unfortunately experienced Adrina spots it, his pained half-grin, which she knows means he'll eventually dump her, like all the others. And we suffer with her as she smiles bigger and talks faster, hoping she's wrong this time, until all we want to do is give her a pool and tell her to relax.

But we can't save her because we know she's got to save herself. Instead of giving her the chance to make it right with her beau, we put her on a plane to Australia, where for a long time she looks down on all that water. The jet is exchanged for a six-seater and we again find Adrina gazing down upon a wavy ocean, though this time it consists of bleached, baked earth.

Having grown alongside Adrina, we never look at shy kids, the socially awkward or workaholics in a shallow, dismissive way ever again, having learned that everyone has a reason for being who they are.

We've grown so much, in fact, that when the plane crashes five minutes from now, it will be as if we crash, too.

Your Character

Exercise 8: What You're Learning

It's time to consider what you've learned about yourself from your character. Open your project's file and begin a new document titled *Diary, Journal, Think Log* or whatever you find appropriate. Then after every writing session, jot down thoughts spurred by your character's development. These entries can be long, elaborate descriptions of how you're feeling at every step of your character's development, or simply a list of brief notes, whether funny, serious or otherwise. What bothers you? What do you find challenging? What's driving you nuts? What do you think about your character? What has she taught you?

This is your opportunity to emote so you don't unintentionally bog down your book with your own personal baggage. You can decide later whether your insights or feelings have a legitimate place in your story.

Such an entry might look like this:

Think Log (11/9) — It's amazing how much Vietnamese iced coffee I make Adrina drink. Poor woman. No wonder she's so nervous. But I love that stuff, the concentrated shot of caffeine, the thick layer of sweet and condensed milk at the bottom. But what bothers me is how she doesn't drink it all. She's always rushing off without that last sip, which is exactly what my sister used to do. Never fully enjoying the moment. And in the desert, I've decided no snakes. I know if it's a desert you've got to have a snake attack, but I just can't do it. Though maybe this is a good chance to overcome my aversion to reptiles. My neighbor is always offering to let me pet his boa constrictor…. But seriously, I feel bad Adrina's dad reminds me so much of mine. I didn't mean that to happen, but it did.

Imbuing our characters with life experience and compassion will make both our characters and us more interesting. Yet what will upgrade us all from interesting to fascinating is not only how much we feel, but also how much we know.

Which begs the question, how much do we know?

Chapter 9
Cultivating Credibility

Imagine we invite people over to gaze upon a beautiful plant we've grown, explaining that its magnificence is due to our expertise as gardeners.

Then someone asks, "How interesting. What is it?"

And we say, "It's a plant. As you can see, it has stems, leaves —"

"Yes, but what is it? What's its name? What family does it belong to? What are its special properties?"

And we say, "Uh…"

The jig up, they'll wander off, unimpressed.

A pitiable story, the bright side is that it does not have to be our story. Not, that is, if we understand a basic rule of readership: people don't simply want to be told a character possesses certain knowledge, they want proof.

That means besides adding our emotions and personal experience, the best way to nourish our character — and make her credible — is by proving she knows everything she's supposed to about her job, hobbies, where she lives, etc., which in turn will prove we know what we're doing.

The Proper Research

Say our protagonist is a sailor and we write a scene in which she gets ready for a voyage by "doing things." Once at sea, a storm arrives and "gives her a hard time." When she gets into harbor, "she docks."

Have we convinced readers the character is a skilled sailor, or do our vague descriptions prove we don't know a thing about boats and neither does our heroine? If the latter, readers won't find her credible even if she's got a fantastic defining detail and a clear motivation. That and they'll have a hard time getting engaged in the story if they can't visualize the character's actions. "She got onto her boat" is not nearly as compelling as

> *Kenda trots up the gangplank and onto the polished deck of the fully refurbished 205-foot, three-mast schooner named Elena, built in 1874. Striding past one of two cargo hatches toward the raised fo'c's'le deck, she shades her eyes against the noonday sun and looks up through the rigging, judging the wind to be about five knots.*

If your character is a real person, she's got a wealth of information from what she's learned in life so far. Use that to convince readers she is who she claims to be. If she sails a schooner, she should know the difference between a gaff and a gimball. If he's a genealogy enthusiast of Belgian origin, he should be proud of his great, great, great grandfather, Baudouin Grossard from the Luxembourg province of Wallonia. If she's a weaver, she should know how to card, when to hook, why to spin and whether to twin or twill.

Point made, it's time to determine everything your character should know in order to appear believable. Some you'll already know from your own experiences, while the rest you'll have to research.

Two Approaches

When researching, you can use either or both of the following approaches: *all-around research* or *scene-specific research*.

All-around research: All-around research means doing a thorough study of any subject the character should know in-depth. If our schooner captain works at a maritime museum on the East Coast, she should know a lot about schooners, the East Coast maritime history and how a maritime museum operates.

The advantage of in-depth research is that you'll learn a tremendous amount, and presumably about subjects you enjoy, or you wouldn't have chosen them for your character. Your study will also give you a lot of ideas for scenes, appropriate symbolism and all aspects of character development. Becoming knowledgeable about the story's main topic is also likely to convince publishers to buy your story, since you obviously know what you're talking about. Lastly, you'll be better equipped to promote your work through articles and lectures.

The main disadvantage of in-depth research is that it's time-consuming and can be unnecessary, especially if you only need one piece of information to make a scene authentic. If we're writing a story about a gangster in 1932 Chicago and want to include a description of his getaway car, does it make sense to research all of automotive history?

No, which brings us to scene-specific research.

Scene-specific research: Scene-specific research consists of finding a few specific facts that, while not particularly important to the overall story, can make a scene memorable and authentic.

Consider our story about the Chicago gangster. A former banker and proud Irishman, we do an all-around research on both topics, as well as the weaponry he uses in his life of crime. We compile our scenes and begin writing. When we come to the gangster's escape, we realize that because the police witness the event, they'll have a description of the car, which means we need one, too.

We can insert a note about the fact we need and continue writing, such as, "Gerald ran out of the bank, the money-stuffed briefcase under his arm and jumped into the getaway car (find out what kind)." Or we can do a quick search on 1932 automobiles by looking through a book, calling an antique car museum or consulting the Internet. When we find what we want — a fast, flashy, shiny black Ford Cabriolet with white-wall tires — we can drop the detail into place and keep writing. This approach is preferable, especially if we know the research will only take a few minutes, since what we learn can alter how we write the scene. Whereas if we insert the fact later, we'll probably have to do some rewriting.

While scene-specific research is fast and effective if you know what you need and where to find it, you'll probably have to do some all-around research, too. If unsure about which approach to use and when, ask yourself, *Is the subject integral to the story or not?* If it is, do all-around research. If it's not, scene-specific will probably suffice.

Volume

If you like research and are particularly proud of your thorough effort, you'll be tempted to use all the information you find. Doing so, however, could slow the pace of your story, overwhelm your readers, give them the impression you're showing off or that you have no idea how to edit. So before using any fact, ask yourself, *Does the detail make the scene or character authentic?* If not, leave it out. You can always use excess material in articles, lectures and other promotional efforts.

Research can also give you a good reason to avoid writing, especially if you find the former easier than the latter. Granted, it's easy to get lost in research, given a few minutes spent reading a book or surfing the web can turn into hours.

If you're prone to either trap, set aside what you believe is a realistic amount of time for initial research, whether an hour, day, week, month or several months. When that time is up, start writing no matter what. You can always continue to research as you write, though make sure fact-finding doesn't take up more than a small percentage — 10 percent or so — of your daily writing time.

Dialogue

If we're writing about characters who come from different regions and eras with which we're unfamiliar, dialogue is a necessary part of research. Without it, our characters may sound like idiots. Imagine we're from England and, having decided to write about an 1800s Appalachian Mountain man, come up with such dialogue as, "Hey y'all. I'm looking forward to this deer hunt. It should be brilliant. And it'll help pay my son's way through university. By the way, could you hold my gun for a sec? I've got to use the loo." Hardly convincing.

Even if we think we know the proper dialect, we should still do research to keep from falling prey to stereotypes, or what we think all southern country people sound like, such as, "Well dabnabbit, you Yankee schemer, by gol I'll wring that thar neck if you don't a-hold this a-here shotgun while I go a-water a tree down the ways a-piece." Now compare the two previous examples to something more authentic: "Don't argie with me, Clay. A body'd be afeared of dyin afore he could crost this holler feelin' puny as I do. Sit in that chur a spell and I'll be back afore that head of yourn manages one good idee."

When researching dialogue, think about the four aspects that make spoken language unique among individuals as well as among various regional, cultural or social groups: *pronunciation, sentence structure, slang* and *speech signatures.*

Pronunciation: As we talked about in *Chapter 2*, pronunciation refers to the way a person forms his words. Does he say *about* with his mouth round and wide, so the word rhymes with *shout*, or does he keep his mouth closed tight so it comes out *a-boot*? Does she say fried chicken as it's spelled, or does she change the vowels so it comes out *frod cheekin*?

People often pronounce certain words in unusual ways due to personality quirks. Consider those who either subconsciously or purposely alter the names of people they don't like, so that Robert — who likes to be called Robert — becomes Bob-o to his passive-aggressive brother-in-law. If such alterations are consistent, they form patterns. Patterns can also be learned — that's just how people talk in that region — or be the result of physical or neurological origins, like a profound hearing loss.

Once we understand how our characters pronounce words, how do we convey that pronunciation to our readers?

The most obvious way is to shorten or phonetically spell the words so readers can see how they're being pronounced, such as *'ol* instead of *old*. While this helps readers hear the dialogue in their heads, phonetically-spelled sentences can be challenging to read: "Ha tolt 'im ha'd'do dat soon's s'ha finishes heya," ("I told him I would do that as soon as I finished here.").

If you feel such manipulation of words is necessary to help readers hear how your character speaks, and so understand him better — his origin, physical challenges or peculiarities — then do so. Readers will catch on so long as your character's dialogue remains consistent without being too obviously consistent. People who say *ain't*, for example, will sometimes say *don't* instead.

Readers catch on to altered spelling and word usage even quicker if they're submerged in it. Think of Shakespearean characters who speak Elizabethan, a form of English that can at first look and sound incomprehensible. Yet the more you read, the more patterns of usage emerge until you find yourself understanding the story.

If you don't want readers stopping to figure out what a character has said, use the traditional spelling of words and then explain how the character pronounces them, such as, "'I told you I didn't want to do it,' he said, *didn't* coming out *din.*" You can even describe the characteristics of an accent and let readers' imaginations do the rest, as in, "When he spoke in his native African dialect, it sounded like a series of metallic pings and clicks, as though someone were flicking a soda can."

Sentence structure: You can convey information about your character via the way he structures his sentences.

If he says, "Do you want to come with?" as opposed to, "Do you want to come?" or "Do you want to come with us," he's probably from Illinois or some nearby Midwestern state. If he says, "I no go with you," instead of, "I will not go with you," then he probably does not speak English as a first language.

Using proper sentence structure as a comparison, listen to how people change that structure. Do they put the adjective after the noun as happens in Spanish, such as *la casa blanca*, which literally means *the house white?* Do they end every sentence with a question, such as, "I didn't want to, you know what I'm saying? It's like, why should I put up with it?" Do they drop verbs so that "How are you doing?" becomes, "How you doing?" Do they rely on one- and two-word sentences like, "So? Who cares? Forget it."

Slang and colloquialisms: Slang can tell a lot about people, including their age, where they were born and what social groups they belong to.

Regarding age, if you know what *Big Daddy* and *backseat bingo* mean (older person and necking in a car, respectively), you probably came of age in the 1950s. If you know how to *potch a pike* and *drink sack*, you're either a historian or like to dress up as a 1400s peasant and attend Medieval fairs.

Regarding place of birth, if you're from Wisconsin, you're a cheesehead. If you're from Alaska, *going outside* means leaving the state.

If you call New Orleans (N'awlins) home, a *banquette* is not a dinner celebration, but rather a sidewalk.

Regarding social groups or organizations, if you're a U.S. Marine, you're a *jarhead*. If you're a ballet dancer, you don't take a class, you *take class*.

Colloquialisms are an offshoot of slang. Informal sayings or expressions, they're often born of cultures within particular regions. If you're in the military, you know *cocked, locked and ready to rock* means prepared for anything, the saying grounded in the tough, cool weapons culture in which soldiers cock their M-16s, lock the bolt forward and set the switch to AUTO, making their rifles fully automatic and ready.

Speech signatures: Speech signatures are the words, sayings or patterns that make each person's speech unique. Consider someone who often adds *yes* to the end of her sentences. "I told him to go away and that was wrong, yes? I didn't want to, yet I had to, yes?" And there are those who repeat favorite phrases, such as "*I'll show him to* charge me extra. I told him I was taking it to a judge. *I'll show him to* take advantage of people." Then there are those who add something to every name they utter. "Danny boy! Susie baby! Judy honey!"

Using speech signatures is the best way to assure that every character sounds unique. To test whether you've succeeded, list a portion of each character's dialogue on one document without including the characters' names. Then have people familiar with your story read the snippets. If they can determine who's talking, you've done a great job.

A Caution: Think carefully about whether you're applying the rules of one character's dialogue to all the characters in the story. If not, you could wind up unintentionally insulting a segment of your readers.

Say we're writing a book about a community of poor, uneducated Hispanic immigrants in America. If we use phonetic spelling and shortened words to depict their speech, readers won't object because the rule is uniformly applied. The protagonist talks that way, as does his sister and the grocer down the block.

But let's say our story features four Caucasians and one Hispanic, all of whom are poor and uneducated, yet we only use altered dialogue for the Hispanic, perhaps because we've fallen prey to cliché or are fascinated by the Hispanic character's way of talking and want to convey our enthusiasm. Although neither reason is mean-spirited, readers might interpret the variation in dialogue styles as a slight; that by singling out the only Hispanic character for such treatment, the author is ridiculing Hispanics, or at least implying they're somehow inferior to whites of the same socioeconomic status.

Fiction Example:

A fabulous example of how the right dialogue can make a regional story sing is *Jack and the Fire Dragon,* a children's story by Gail E. Haley. The tale tells of how Jack of Jack and the Beanstalk fame set up a homestead with his two brothers, only to be set upon by Old Fire Dragaman, a wicked giant who roams the hills, his eyes a snaky green. Whenever he disappears into his underground cave, he morphs into a fire-breathing dragon.

Haley uses everything — shortened words, phonetic spelling, slang and colloquialisms — to capture the sing-song quality of old days Appalachian Mountain speech. Jack is a reckless *feller* who says *Bedad!* His mother tells her boys to clear land for each of *ye.* But what makes the book so terrific is that Haley carries the rhythm of the dialogue over into the narrative, creating a magical, dark cadence as rolling as the landscape where the story takes place.

Nonfiction Example:

A book that clearly illustrates the all-around research approach is *The Explosive Child: A New Approach for Understanding and Parenting Easily Frustrated, Chronically Inflexible Children* by Ross W. Greene. The book is aimed at helping parents understand and cope with kids so inflexible in their thinking they're prone to sudden, explosive outbreaks of temper.

Just by reading Greene's various professional titles, you get an idea of how deeply he's researched the topic of chronically inflexible kids over the course of his career: he's director of Cognitive-Behavioral Psychology at the Clinical and Research Program in Pediatric Pharmacology at Massachusetts General Hospital and an associate clinical professor of psychology in Harvard Medical School's Department of Psychiatry. His material is not only drawn from one-on-one work with parents and their children, but also studies he's performed within his field.

Though impressive credentials, what proves his expertise is that rather than cram the book with statistics, bar graphs and long titles of various studies, he focuses almost exclusively on patients he's treated over the years. He opens the book by relating an incident involving an 11-year-old girl who had a serious meltdown over something as miniscule as frozen waffles.

Greene's approach goes back to what we learned in *Chapter 1*, that stories are, at their most fundamental level, about people. Discover how your story impacts peoples' lives and you'll find your readers.

How to Research

Read, View, Listen

Of all research methods, reading is the most obvious way to gather information. And don't just think in terms of library books. If you want the flavor of a corporate accountant's life and need to slip accounting lingo into your narrative, look over a corporate accounting manual. If your character's car breaks down and he's a mechanic, read a car manual. Peruse cookbooks, foreign newspapers and poetry your character might enjoy. Look over anatomical diagrams and financial statements. Read travel books to learn about places your character visits. Study political manifestos and legal documents for the language used therein. Go over screenplays known for excellent dialogue. Look up government documents pertaining to health statistics, guidelines for submitting a bill to Congress and the process for applying to West Point.

Besides reading, you can view and/or listen to recorded materials such as how-to DVDs, audio books, poetry readings, speeches, video clips of news events or movies that pertain to your subject.

Fortunately, research material is easier, faster and cheaper to get due to the Internet. Rather than spend weeks or months seeking information through the mail, many documents, reports and applications are now available online. You can also find song lyrics, obscure maps, foreign language dictionaries, video clips, ancient texts, commentary from experts around the world and even the e-mail addresses of those experts should you have questions.

So if you don't yet have a computer or Internet access, consider purchasing both or going to libraries featuring those services. If you have Internet access but don't know how to use it, take a web surfing class or ask a more experienced friend for help.

That said, while the Internet is a great way to research, it's also rife with bogus information. People routinely email "true" online stories that are actually the work of pranksters or marketing people. So be sure to trace information back to a verifiable source before using it in your work.

Interview

If reading is the most obvious way to research, in-person interviews are the most satisfying since talking to people allows you to collect not only their knowledge, but also information pertaining to the five senses. You can hear people's accents, study their facial expressions and note their scent. You can shake their hands and otherwise touch related items, such as photos and artifacts they collected during world travels.

Meeting someone also allows you to change locations during the interview. If you talk to a master gardener at her home, for example, she might invite you to take a walk through her garden while pointing to plants, imparting her expertise and answering questions, a sensory experience no book could give you. Nor could a book/CD/DVD answer specific questions regarding your character's particular situation. If you're writing a murder mystery and chose a plant with which to kill your literary victim, you could ask the master gardener her opinion. She might say it's a bad choice, list the reasons why and then refer you to something more suitable while walking you over to the specimen and explaining everything you need to know.

If you visit people enough, they usually get used to you and begin telling you things they never intended to mention. To build such rapport, be courteous and come prepared with appropriate questions. If your story could significantly impact them, let them know that and be sure to give them fair warning of the story's publication, which is known as a courtesy call.

If you can't interview someone in person, you can do a phone interview, which will still allow you to ask specific questions and analyze the interviewee's speech.

Gain Firsthand Experience

If your character is a daredevil adventurer, why should he have all the fun? After all, if you try some of the things he does, you'll not only have a great time, but you'll also make your character's actions 90 percent more authentic. So go bungee jumping, try parasailing, make time to scuba dive with the stingrays.

Gaining firsthand experience can also mean taking lessons and visiting locales important to your character. If he plays the tabla, an Indian instrument consisting of two drums, take some tabla lessons. If your character came from a tiny South Dakota town on the edge of the Black Hills, go visit to understand where she came from.

Besides adding depth to your character and color and intensity to scenes, firsthand experience allows you to test your ideas. If you're writing a crime caper that takes place in downtown L.A. and need to know whether the escape is realistic, try traveling the route at the time of day specified in your book. You might find there's too much traffic and need to change the time or route.

Keep Excellent Records

Open your project's file and create a document titled *Research Sources*. As you research, record the source of everything you read, everyone you talk to and everything you learn through firsthand experience.

Reading material: List everything about the source (title, author, web site, etc.): page numbers; a copy of the information you're using; hard copy printouts; photos. Include anything that will help you find the material again and write accurate supporting documents, such as a bibliography. If you want to use copyrighted information, like quotes from someone's book, you'll need that detailed information when submitting a request for permission to use the material.

Interviews: List as much information as possible about the people you interview (name, age, contact information, place of employment, etc.): list details about the meeting itself (where it took place, the time, who was in attendance, etc.); take notes during the interview via a laptop or notebook; file notes with other hard copy information so it doesn't get lost. Include everything necessary to contact the interviewee again, either to confirm information or alert him of the publication date, and thank him for his help via a personal note or on the acknowledgments page of your story.

Firsthand experience: Record everything about the setup of the experience (time of day, weather, contact person, outfitter, location, other people in attendance, cost, etc.): describe the experience in detail (how long it took, what you learned, the exact name of any materials used, the interactions among people, etc.); the contact information for experts or other participants, should you need clarification about something while writing. Again, don't worry about an overflow of information. What you don't use in your main writing project can be used to market your work.

Fiction Example:

Whether we love the classic *Little House* series by Laura Ingalls Wilder or find the stories about pioneer life too quiet for our big action preferences, none of us can deny the authenticity of the information conveyed in the books, from clothes, church hymns and social interactions to food, prairie weather and descriptions of farm life. That's because Wilder was writing from firsthand experience. Born in 1867 rural Wisconsin, Wilder fictionalized her family's adventures as they moved to Kansas, Minnesota and South Dakota.

In *Little House on the Prairie*, Ma wakes up Laura and Mary when it's time to leave for Minnesota. Instead of simply "getting them ready," Wilder uses three sentences of detail to authenticate the time period and set the scene. Ma washes and combs their hair by candlelight and firelight because it's still dark and cold. She dresses them in red flannel long johns; wool petticoats, dresses and stockings; coats with rabbit-skin hoods; and knitted mittens of red yarn. Pa packs his fiddle-box and the kids breakfast on bread and molasses.

If we decided to write about pioneer life, we could do an excellent job of researching that time period. We might come upon and use the word *fiddle-box* and accurately explain where Pa hangs his gun, bullet pouch and powder horn on the covered wagon. But what would be harder to accomplish is the way Wilder conveys the social mores of her time. In short, she doesn't explain them at all. Having lived during that period in history, she assumes other people share her viewpoint so there's no need to explain, an outlook that's difficult to achieve through research.

For example, when the family comes upon other travelers, either friendly or threatening, the girls say nothing. The pattern is so consistent that readers come to understand the reason: when in the presence of adults, children of that time truly were reared to be *seen and not heard*, as the saying goes. Nor did children talk back to adults, even when kids hated what they were being asked to do.

As contemporary writers, we might feel obligated to explain the social dynamics, because if we find 1870s frontier society somewhat foreign, we'll assume our readers do, too. We might also unwittingly apply our standards of society to the period we're talking about, a common mistake in historically-based fiction. Instead of a quiet, obedient child as Wilder depicts, our Laura might resemble a kid of today; one who speaks to adults whenever she feels like it and objects when she doesn't want to do something.

Lastly, we might feel pressured to use politically correct terms, whereas Wilder apparently felt no such obligation. The Wilders headed into land occupied by Indians, not Native Americans.

Does lack of firsthand experience mean you shouldn't undertake stories set in historical time periods? No. It means you should attempt to interview someone with firsthand experience, and if that's not possible, imagine yourself as a member of that time period. What would you wear, eat and say? How would you greet someone or think of honor and love? As you write, keep the explanation of your character's attitude to a minimum. Readers will catch on faster than you think regarding the societal rules that regulate your characters' behavior.

Nonfiction Example:

In *The Perfect Storm*, Sebastian Junger employs an impressive amount of all-around research to explain the last days of six men aboard the Andrea Gail, a swordfishing vessel that disappeared in October of 1991 in the North Atlantic Ocean during a vicious Nor'easter.

Junger researched the men's lives, the swordfishing industry off the New England coast, swordfish boats, ocean currents in the North Atlantic and meteorological and historical background of the area. He also interviewed a lot of people, including those close to the six men and those who survived the storm and performed search and rescue operations.

The combination of technical detail and personal stories creates an enthralling story built on a crescendo of weather that ends with a storm sporting 70-foot rogue waves, hurricane force winds and swells strong enough to back up the Hudson River for a hundred miles.

Character Study 9

To make Adrina more credible, we'll list everything she should know and where we might look for the information:

Vietnamese values, culture, language: We can check out web sites, books and CDs/tapes, visit a Vietnamese community in San Jose and interview residents, and read Vietnamese poetry. Specifically, we can gather information about local celebrations, street names and other details of where she grew up; visit online English-to-Vietnamese translation sites for symbolic phrases; record and study the speech patterns of Vietnamese immigrants; listen to library tapes for proper pronunciation of Vietnamese words.

Water: We can view web sites and books and interview hydrogeologists. Specifically, we can research the properties of water, how and where it flows through the earth, and interesting statistics that could be symbolically used to parallel Adrina's physical and mental state as it changes.

Desert survival skills learned from Adrina's fieldwork in the Kalahari: We can view web sites and books while interviewing experts. Specifically, we need information about where she worked in the Kalahari and what she learned from the natives.

Australia: We'll view maps, read books and web sites and perform interviews, either by email, phone or in-person. We'll also visit if time and money permit. Specifically, we need to know: the source of water for various regions; everything about the outback, from the smells and sounds to physical features, contours of the land and colors at various times of the day; the expertise of those who live in or near the outback; an appropriate location for the crash; the distance from the crash to civilization.

Small passenger planes: We'll peruse photos, web sites and books while interviewing experts who fly in desert environments. Specifically, we'll need details regarding: features of the plane; inside layout including seating configuration and exits; and a good reason the plane might crash (mechanical problems, weather conditions, collision of some sort, etc.).

We'll add new research headings as necessary. When most of the main topics have been identified, anything that pops up can probably be handled through scene-specific research.

Your Character

Exercise 9: What Does Your Character Need to Know?

Open your project's file and create a new document titled *Research*. Using our character study as an example, begin listing everything your character will need to know to seem credible. Be sure to keep a neat record of your research by organizing it as such until you establish your own system:

1. general topic
2. where to find the information
3. subtopics, or specific information you'll need
4. research sources (all specific details related to the source should be recorded on your *Research Sources* worksheet)
5. results of research

Imagine we're writing a nonfiction book about the Randolph family of Williamsburg, VA, and will be using Colonial American weaving as a vehicle for telling our story. Here's what our research document might look like. The numbers will help you identify the various research components:

(1) **Williamsburg.** I can: (2) visit Williamsburg; look at historical maps, books and web sites; interview experts; and take weaving lessons. (3) Specifically, I need to know who populated the town in 1772, the politics of the region at that time and popular weaving methods and patterns.

(3) <u>Basic history</u>
(4) Official Colonial Williamsburg web site: (www.williamsburg…)
(5) capital of Virginia from 1699 to 1780

(3) <u>People Who Lived There in 1772</u>
(4) Official Colonial Williamsburg web site: (www.williamsburg…)
(5) Randolph family: Peyton, born 1721, presided over the Continental Congress, died 1775, friend of George Washington, son of influential Sir John and Lady Susannah Randolph

(3) <u>Weaving in Colonial America</u>
(4) National Gallery of Art web site:
(5) From late 1600s to 1850 woven bed covers (called coverlets) were popular; overshot weave was popular and consisted of a warp yarn (2-ply linen or cotton), binder weft (single ply) and pattern weft (colored yarn).

Needless to say, finding out as much as you can will not only make you more knowledgeable about your character, but will deepen readers' appreciation for your character's complexity and know-how.

While such research may give you the impression you're ready to present your character to the public, you have to be sure he'll be viewed in the best possible light from the moment readers meet him.

Because like it or not, first impressions count.

Chapter 10
A Carefully Tended First Impression

Although most of us wish people would ignore first impressions and get to know us for who we are instead of what we look like, few of us actually practice what we preach. Like it or not, we're just as susceptible to first impressions as the next person.

First impressions are usually based on appearance because sight allows us to glean a lot of information quickly and so know what to expect. If a well-groomed man smiles as he walks toward us, we assume he's not a threat, whereas if a foul-smelling person wearing a maniacal grin approaches, we'll steer clear, given we don't know what he's capable of.

Readers' first impressions of a character can be just as immediate and strong, which means be very conscious of the way you introduce him since that may be what readers remember most.

Why Introductions Matter

Reader Expectations

Even if we learn that a person is not as snooty and tight-lipped as we first thought, our initial impression never leaves us; that perhaps the smirk we saw on her face the first time we met says something important about her, something that may come into play later in the relationship.

Readers are often similarly affected. They assume that if you're introducing the character in a certain way, it's because you're trying to tell them something important about the character, which you should be. Specifically, you should, in one precisely described moment, convey your character's role in the story. That will tell readers why she's worth reading about, which will help them set appropriate expectations. If you introduce someone as a side character, readers will only expect so much from her, whereas if you introduce her as a main character, they'll expect a lot more.

Conveying your character's role during a first introduction does not mean telling readers everything there is to know about him, a problem we'll talk about in a moment. Nor does it mean resorting to clichés, such as giving your character a thin black mustache so they'll know he's an antagonist. Rather, focus on the following three factors: *the introduction's length, placement within the story* and *style*.

Length

An introduction is often most effective when it's no more than one or two sentences long. If that seems incredibly short, consider that's what happens in real conversation. When talking to other people, we don't normally say, "I went with Gretchen. She's the tall black woman I went to school with, the one with the tattoo of a skull and crossbones on her ankle. She was originally a business major and then changed to medieval history. She comes from a family of scientists, yet she's all into voodoo. She lights candles when she does her own show at the student radio station...."

While all interesting stuff, we instinctively know that if our description goes on for too long, we'll lose our audience. So when introducing a character, do it quickly and get on with the story, such as, "I went with Gretchen, that tall black woman I went to college with, the one with the skull and crossbones tattoo. We took off at midnight...." Having explained her role (accomplice) and given a precise detail to make her memorable (the tattoo), we can begin the story.

Now let's go back to our Alaskan Bubba. We'll introduce him via a first-person narrator, who sits in a darkened bar. Looking sideways, the narrator sees "a flash of white teeth and the glint of a heavy coin twirling down the bar like a dancer spun about and let go. By the time the coin clatters to a heap before me, the man and his laughter are gone." Because it's a sharply focused moment, readers will understand it's significance, that whoever spun that coin will be the focal point of the story even though only represented by a flash of teeth, glint of whirling metal and the sound of laughter. Note that the character's name was not even mentioned.

Placement

The placement of an introduction refers to where the character shows up in the story, the beginning, middle or end. In most cases, important characters, such as the protagonist, antagonist and key support characters, show up in the first third of the story, while support and side characters can be introduced throughout the book.

Once readers know the main players and their connection to one another, readers can submerge themselves in the story and stay there until the end. Conversely, waiting to introduce significant characters requires readers to pull themselves out of the story in order to figure how the new character fits in.

Now let's take a closer look at actual placement. Imagine a 300-page book about a young World War II soldier who falls in love with a woman. They marry and on page 200, he goes off to war. A few pages later, the woman opens her door to find two men in military dress, their faces grim. Because readers are two-thirds into the book, well after all significant characters have been introduced, they'll expect these two men to be side characters and probably catalysts who have arrived to deliver bad news and so up the tension of the story.

Now imagine the book opens on the morning after the soldier and his wife got married following a whirlwind courtship. They hear a knock on their door and open up to find the two men in military dress. Because it's only page three, readers will pay close attention to this introduction. Sure enough, the men serve a warrant for the soldier's arrest regarding a criminal matter that occurred a month previous in a bar halfway around the world. Given the placement of the introduction and the context, we know the men will be antagonists.

Style

By carefully choosing the style of introduction, or how a person is introduced, you can get readers to see the character as you do.

If you want to convey a young woman's breezy, restless temperament, you can introduce her in a breezy way:

> *The wind was warm that day and scented by wet hay and mud from spring rain, the wildflowers growing in the puddled ditch as Wendy hitched herself down the gravel road at a skip, the ends of her hair dancing.*

Likewise, if you want to reflect a character's direct manner, you can choose a direct introduction, such as, "He turned and found himself staring into the black eyes of the woman he most wanted to avoid, Mrs. Stringer." You can even introduce a character indirectly through other characters, as in, "Sally glared at the ground and said, 'Everything would have been okay if *she* hadn't come.'" Again, you don't have to use the character's name. Nor does the character have to be present at the time of introduction.

You can use a different style to introduce each character. Or you can use the same style for all characters in order to give the story an overall feel. If you want the story to reflect the obsessive/compulsive nature of the narrator, you could have him introduce everyone via his cleanliness scale of one (filthiest) to 10 (cleanliest), the postman a two due to how much dirty mail he handles, while the narrator's chiropractor rates a 10 for his exceptional air recirculation system.

Or say you want to create the feel of a spy mission and so make every introduction like the clicking of a spy camera meant to record every detail:

> *The shiny gold doors of the casino's penthouse suite opened and out walked Bob "The Nose" Kincaid. Hook-shaped scar on his left cheek. Partial left ear. Black eyes. The nose: bulbous, pocked, red. He wore Lefty Dean and Marzden Hertz on either flank.*

You can also use a particular style of introduction to convey how a character sees himself. If the character is honest and self-aware, the portrayal can be as candid. If the character has a distorted self-image, or a good reason to hide his true nature, the portrayal may be deceiving. The character could at first appear to be an antagonist and turn out to be a protagonist, or vice versa. Readers won't mind being surprised so long as you have a good reason to deceive them. Consider a man who swaggers into a Las Vegas casino, a diamond ring on his right pinky and a bodyguard nearby. From the readers' viewpoint, this guy sees himself as The Man; the hottest of hotshots, the grandest of God's gift to women, the supreme top banana. Then as the story unfolds, it turns out he's an eccentric, comical guy who happens to have a lot of money. Then again, maybe it's all an act and he's really an undercover G-man attempting to draw out a particular big spender. Whatever you choose, remember that literary introductions have as much style — and power — as introductions we experience in our own lives.

Fiction Example:

Harper Lee's *To Kill a Mockingbird* is narrated by a girl named Scout Finch, who recounts the summer a boy named Dill came to visit their small Alabama town during the Great Depression. The newcomer gives Scout and her older brother, Jem, a reason to talk about a strange member of their neighborhood:

> *Inside the house lived a malevolent phantom. People said he existed, but Jem and I had never seen him. People said he went out at night when the moon was down, and peeped in windows. When people's azaleas froze in a cold snap, it was because he had breathed on them. Any stealthy small crimes committed in Maycomb were his work. Once the town was terrorized by a series of morbid nocturnal events: people's chickens and household pets were found mutilated; although the culprit was Crazy Addie, who eventually drowned himself in Barker's Eddy, people still looked at the Radley Place, unwilling to discard their initial suspicions.*

The malevolent phantom turns out to be Boo Radley, who Jem describes as 6-and-a-half feet tall with bloodstained hands from eating raw squirrels, a jagged scar across his face, yellowed and rotting teeth and popped eyes.

Boo is mentioned on page nine, so we know he'll be significant. The length of the entire introduction comes to two paragraphs. And judging by his ferocious description, he's an antagonist, an impression that could be true or not. Lastly, he's introduced via a spooky Halloween style, which is fitting since the climax takes place on a windy, creepy October night as Jem and Scout wander home from a Halloween play at their school.

Nonfiction Example:

Let's return to Flora Rheta Schreiber's book, *Sybil*, about the woman who created 16 different personalities to deal with the psychological and physical abuse she endured as a child.

Schreiber introduces Sybil via shattering glass, a sound so intimately tied to her tortured past that an act as simple as a dropped beaker in her chemistry class at Columbia University terrifies her enough to send her into a psychotic episode.

The sharp, dramatic style of the seven-sentence introduction also helps set the tone of the book; that this will be a dramatic story about a woman in major crisis.

The Method of Introduction

If style is how a character is introduced, then method refers to the way in which a character is introduced.

A Physical Description

The most popular way to introduce characters is via their physical descriptions as we did when introducing Bob "The Nose" Kincaid. Yet because it's the most popular method, it's also the most overused. Therefore, if tempted to use this strategy, be sure the description tells something about your character beyond what he looks like. If showing readers how a character eats a plate of spaghetti — voraciously and with a disgusting level of mess — both explains his upcoming role in the book and symbolizes how he handles competitors, then use it. The same is true if you describe the way a kid stares at people with his light gray, almost white eyes, in order to establish a properly sinister tone.

But if you find yourself introducing your character via his appearance out of habit or because you don't know any other strategies, it's time to consider other approaches.

Via the Defining Detail

Introducing a character via her defining detail has the advantage of letting readers know immediately what's most important about her.

If the defining detail comes from a situation, you can describe the event as a way to set up the main story. Say you use the first few paragraphs of your story to describe the moment a small boy realizes he can't trust adults. Then you can skip ahead to the character's teen years and be assured readers will understand his basic bias against adults.

You can also introduce a character via a defining detail based on an object, prominent physical characteristic or imagined blemish. You can describe the way she allows her long hair to hide the strawberry birthmark on her cheek, or talk about the odd track of muddy footprints left by a character who suffered from childhood polio.

Again, don't feel obligated to fully explain the defining detail. After a few sentences or paragraphs, move on. You can always go back — once, twice or as many times as necessary — to flesh out the significance of what you first mentioned.

Through Dialogue/Monologue

Dialogue is a great way to introduce characters because it's fast, entertaining and can create suspense. For example:

"I can't, I just… can't."

"I warned you, I — Oh, the hell with it! All this time.
Messing around, waiting for you — I'm calling Mr. Lipinski."

"No!"

"What do you mean, no —"

"You can't. He'll —"

"Don't tell me what I can't do! I'm calling. It's not like
I wanted to. You think I wanted this? You made me.
You forced me to!"

We don't know anything about Mr. Lipinski, yet we understand he'll
be an important character, and judging by the threat with which his
name is uttered, probably an antagonist. Having communicated Mr.
Lipinski's purpose, the introduction also creates suspense. Who is Mr.
Lipinski? Why are people so afraid of him?

While you can employ traditional dialogue, you can also introduce a
character by having him talk to himself, as in, "Daniel stood atop the
building, looking down at the sidewalk ten stories below. 'Well,' he
said, 'if I jump I'll prove I'm an idiot, just as Mary always said. On the
other hand, I can't live without her anymore.'" Or the character can
talk directly to readers, such as, "Well, what do you think? Should I
jump or not?"

This strategy is also a fantastic way to introduce nonfiction characters.
If writing about your life, of which your uncle played an important
part, you can introduce him via the first thing you remember him ever
saying to you: "Kid, you'll be rich as Zeus someday or I'm a monkey's
uncle, which I am anyway, by the looks of you."

You can even introduce your character by quoting from a poignant
speech she once made, whether to her union during a strike or while
accepting a Nobel Prize.

Fiction Example:

Having talked about the use of dialogue/monologue, it seems fitting to bring up the suspense crime novel *The Ax* by Donald E. Westlake. The protagonist, Burke Devore, tells readers in the first sentence that, having never killed anyone, he wishes he could consult someone before he does. Particularly, he wishes he could confer with his long-dead father, a World War II vet. Because he can't, Devore instead poses his questions to readers. How do you know if you can kill somebody? What if you can't until you try?

This is a fascinating introduction because of all it accomplishes. Burke's placement at the beginning of the book identifies him as the protagonist. The style of introduction — one person's angst — sets a lonely, desperate tone. Here's a troubled man who craves help about a serious matter, yet he can't bring himself to talk to anyone, which only increases his isolation while creating a one-way mirror effect. We see his pain and want to help, but he can't see or hear us. We can only watch helplessly as he proceeds with his murderous plans, which produces terrific suspense.

Nonfiction Example:

Truth and Beauty by Ann Patchett is a memoir about her friendship with poet Lucy Grealy beginning in the 1980s.

Patchett begins the book by explaining that after being accepted to the Iowa Writers' Workshop, she got a note from Grealy, who was also accepted. In her note, Grealy asked Patchett if, when she went to Iowa City to arrange accommodations, she could also look for an apartment for Grealy.

One sentence on page two of the book, it seems an offhand introduction. Yet what tells us most about Grealy is Patchett's reaction. She's thrilled by the request, given Grealy is a campus celebrity. Rather than be famous for her looks or wealth, however, Grealy is instead a tiny, sloppily dressed woman facially disfigured by cancer and possessed of an incredible talent for poetry.

Unlike previous examples, Patchett's introduction of Grealy extends through eight long paragraphs that meander over four pages. The approach works, however, because it establishes the feel of a wandering journey, a style that's carried throughout the book.

Beware the Info Dump

An info dump is when writers overwhelm readers by attempting to tell them everything there is to know about a situation or character upon the first introduction. Have you ever read a science fiction story in which, in the first three pages, you get a rundown of the protagonist's complex life while learning about the 17 generations of a colony on a triangle-shaped planet so that by page four you're closing the book and massaging your temples? If so, then you know the feeling of utter confusion.

While it seems logical not to dump too much information on readers all at once, it's harder than you think to refrain from doing so. Your character is alive and growing at a fast clip, which means you're exhilarated, yet frustrated because there's so much to tell you don't know where to begin. When in doubt, return to the general rule of introduction: let readers know your character's role in the story, then move on. Once you correctly place the character within the story, the hard part is done. You can use the rest of the story to dole out facts as needed, which we'll talk more about in the next chapter.

If You Get Stuck

When your character begins to grow, he really grows. While thrilling to watch, such growth can be overwhelming. If you begin to feel overcome by possibilities or get stuck on a certain facet of growth, remember the two greatest strategies for freeing yourself.

Organization

Organization means keeping your story's file and subsequent character worksheets updated as the story evolves. Whenever necessary, create new documents or systems for filing information. And don't be stingy. If breaking up one long document into many smaller ones helps clarify your thinking, do it.

For this book, I began with one document, a worksheet on which I brainstormed what information you might find most helpful. By the time I finished, I had 47 documents that reflected every stage of the process, from the original worksheet through various versions of the outline, contract and manuscript, not to mention research documents, supporting documents (table of contents, glossary, etc.), critiques by colleagues and copyright documents regarding permissions to use quotes. Each document is clearly labeled and every version appropriately numbered. All are included in a file for this particular project, as opposed to being mixed in with the hundreds of other documents from my other projects.

How you choose to organize your project is up to you. You can use an alphabetical system, throw everything into one drawer or even rely on astrology. Whatever you choose, you'll know if it's successful if it makes the writing process easier rather than harder.

Return to the Defining Detail

Don't forget that your character is rooted to one spot by her defining detail. If you get lost, go back to her roots and follow her growth upward to the point where you understand what her next move will be. If you're not sure how to introduce her, for example, return to her defining detail. If it's a necklace made of a white seashell that hangs from a leather cord — a symbol of her selfless loyalty to a long-lost love — we know she'd rather people study the shell rather than focus on her. Our thinking clarified, we now know to introduce her indirectly, via a description of the shell and where it comes from.

Character Study 10

How should we introduce Adrina?

Given she's our protagonist, it goes without saying that we'll introduce her at the beginning of our story. In terms of style, let's choose a direct, harsh approach that reflects both the parched environment in which she eventually finds herself and the barren desert of her inner world. That and such a landscape provides a torturous, ironic contrast to Adrina's expertise on water.

Concerning method, we could introduce Adrina via a physical description, yet that would lack impact since the story has little to do with her physique. So instead, let's convey Adrina's mental dilemma via her defining detail. She wants to be happy, but feels frozen in the unhappiness born the day her mother left.

We open the story with the image of a nameless little girl crying hysterically as she runs down a cracked concrete sidewalk in her underpants. Besides introducing our character, the scene immediately engages readers by establishing a suspenseful mystery. *Who is the little girl? What's she running from? What could be so terrifying?*

We can use that beginning to mirror the end of the story, so that if we start by showing little Adrina running and crying, we can end by showing adult Adrina running and crying.

But why would Adrina be running this time? To get away from something, or get to something? And why is she crying? Out of terror, sadness or happiness? We won't know until Adrina leads us there.

Your Character

Exercise 10: Let's Meet

Open your character's worksheet and create a heading titled *Introduction*. Beneath that, list four subheadings for Length, Placement, Style and Method of Introduction.

While the question of where you'll place the character should be fairly easy to answer, take time to brainstorm regarding the length, style and method of introduction. This should be a free-flowing exercise in which ideas are allowed to stream forth, so stay loose of mind and have fun. When you're done, evaluate each idea for appropriateness.

Here's a sample entry regarding a story about two dueling newsmen:

Introduction

Placement: Since Dalton is the antagonist, he needs to be placed near the opening of the story. And since I want readers to think he's the protagonist for a while — bold, dashing, humorous — I'll introduce him before I introduce George, the real protagonist.

Length: The introduction should be short, almost staccato, like the old newsroom AP wire machines that would type out the latest news flashes.

Style: I want the story to have the feel of a sizzling 1930s big-city newspaper article: fast-paced, sensationalistic, screaming headlines.

That will provide a nice parallel to the big murder trial that Dalton and his rival, George, are covering. Therefore I want all characters introduced as they might be in an article (i.e., "Asst. District Attorney Mel Hannoway, who was called to the case... Eyewitness Mrs. Gertrude Kraus told reporters..."). The only character who will be introduced in a different style will be the woman accused of murder, but I'll deal with her introduction later.

Method of introduction: Dalton could be the subject of conversation between two people on the street. Or I could show his normal, bold entrance in the newsroom. Or I could open the story with his byline emblazoned atop an article he wrote about the murder trial.

When you're done brainstorming, go back to any topics for which you have more than one choice and begin a self-conversation to hash out which idea works best. For example:

Self-conversation

Best method of introduction: Of all three choices, I like the last one best. Beginning with his byline followed by the first few paragraphs of his article about the murder trial will 1) mention his name right away as I wanted, 2) allow his jaunty style of writing to set the tone of the book, and 3) introduce the murder case, thus dropping readers right into the action.

Another option is to write three versions of an introduction to see which you like best. As you work, create new documents to handle whatever subjects no longer pertain just to your character, but to the whole story. For example, we could create a new document titled *Style of Story* where we list all the possible ways we could enhance the busy newsroom style of the story, such as using favorite journalistic words/phrases/jargon from that time period and making chapters short and tight like articles submitted under deadline.

As you work, consider all that you've done so far. Your character is almost fully grown and you've either just chosen, or are on the verge of choosing, the best way to introduce him to readers. As your character's sole protector, the guardian of her health and welfare, it's time to ask, *Is there anything else I can do to make sure my character is well received?*

Chapter 11
Readying for Display

Having just decided on the best way to introduce your character, you're ready to tell her story. But how should you do so? As fast as possible or more slowly?

For the answer, consider your own preferences. If you make the effort to take a special garden tour, do you really want to rush through the event? Or would you rather take your time as a knowledgeable docent explains what you're viewing at a pace that's neither too slow nor too fast, but just right for making your experience fascinating and effortless?

Odds are you'll choose the latter, which is why you should reveal your character over the course of the story rather than all at once.

Why Reveal Characters Slowly

Revealing your character over the course of your story: helps avoid an info dump; creates tension; reveals the character's suffering; and moves the story toward its climax.

Say we open our story with 14-year-old Jason. Given his prominent placement at the beginning of the story, readers will know he's a protagonist. We'll use narrative description and a sparse, journalistic style to introduce him as, hands thrust deep in the pockets of his jeans, we describe how he walks through a forest near his far northern California home in June, just as the rainless summer begins. In subsequent scenes, we show how the number of those hikes increases as the summer wears on; how, more and more, Jason looks up at those towering trees, often stopping to snap off branches of dry, dead bushes; how intently he reads a firefighting magazine.

Then we describe Jason in his room one late August day. He's standing before his dresser. Taped to the wall is a laminated article about a house fire three years ago. Apparently readying for a hike, Jason puts on his watch and slips his wallet into his back pocket. Then he swipes a book of matches off his dresser and shoves them into the front pocket of his jeans.

Consider how Jason changes as each piece of information is revealed, and subsequently, how the tension level increases. At first he seems like a solitary, but nice kid. Considering his apparent love of forests and interest in firefighting, readers think he wants to be a firefighter. But then we mention the article about the house fire and the book of matches. Soon our readers begin to wonder if the kid is an arsonist.

Having made Jason into a puzzle, we continue to give readers pieces of information that help them complete the mystery. The more pieces that fall into place, the more readers understand the real Jason, including why and how he suffers. He hikes alone, sits in his room alone, walks to school alone, so that readers begin to feel the crushing weight of his isolation. Knowing that arson is a crime only increases Jason's agony, in that he can't share how beautiful he finds fire and how free it makes him feel, as if he's watching a living piece of artwork; the bigger and more fabulous the art, the more exhilarating the experience.

As his suffering increases and he becomes more desperate, he takes more desperate actions, which propel the story toward the climax when Jason must face his greatest fear.

Ways to Reveal Your Character

When revealing information about Jason, we used the two most common methods available: showing the character's actions (hiking, reading the firefighting magazine, taking the book of matches), and describing important clues (the way he looks at the trees, the article tacked to his wall). But we can also disperse information through dialogue; reactions of and to the character; the impact of the surrounding social or physical environment on the character; and a character's blind spots.

Dialogue

Dialogue is a great way to reveal facts about your character and how she's changing. She can be a participant in the dialogue or the subject of dialogue among others. Consider the following examples:

Example 1 (character participates in dialogue; purpose, to impart facts):

"Let's walk over the bridge. The Creamery is just on
    the other side. I'll treat you to a scoop of peppermint chip."

"No."

"Aw, come on."

"Not ever."

"Dear sister."

"Yes, dear sister?"

"You've got to get over your fear of heights sometime."

"No I don't. My fear and I are quite happy together."

Eight short sentences, yet the dialogue tells us the protagonist is a female, probably in her 20s or beyond, who fears heights and has a good sense of humor, a sister who cares and a taste for peppermint chip ice cream. Judging by the correct grammar usage, she's also probably educated.

Example 2 (the character is the subject of the dialogue; purpose, to impart facts):

> "I ain't going to the dance with her."

> "Why not?"

> "Why not? What the hell's'a'matter with you? She's a
> foot taller, twenty pounds lighter and smells like cat
> food. I feel like barking every time I see her."

The dialogue gives a clear physical description of the absent character: female, tall, skinny and not too attractive. Besides smelling like cat food, we get the idea she's timid and is easily frightened away. The exchange also reveals what the character must contend with, a rough, unrefined culture in which a majority of males are of the let-me-see-her-teeth-first sort, which instantly makes us empathize with her plight.

Example 3 (the character is the subject of the dialogue; purpose, to show change):

> "I was just passing —"

> "He doesn't want to talk to anyone."

> "Look, Lorraine, let me in. Let me see him. It's been
> three months since he was laid off and I'm saying this
> as his friend —"

> "As someone who's still got a job."

> "I'm still his friend, Lorraine. I'm still his friend and

    friends speak up. So I'm doing that and what I'm
    saying is, first it's, 'Come on in,' then, 'Come in but
    don't stay long, he's not feeling well.' And now it's,
    'Don't come in at all.' You know? I mean you see it,
    right? You see what I mean?"

Through this dialogue, readers can easily picture the situation, even without a physical description. A woman peers through a partially open front door, listening to the man standing on the front stoop. They're both middle-aged, worried, and in the woman's case, bitter. Yet more importantly, readers can envision the woman's husband buried deep within the house, perhaps lying in a darkened room. A man who at first tried to be hopeful the layoff would be temporary and "a good thing, in the long run," but who gradually fell into what's become an alarming depression.

Clearly dialogue can impart an enormous amount of information. Just be sure it shows something that simple narrative can't, such as the way a character speaks and how he communicates with other people. If you only use dialogue to impart information, you risk creating an info dump. For example:

> "You know, Judy, that I joined the Women's Foundation because I was proud of it's heritage; how it was founded in 1871 by Phyllis Dindorf as a refuge for women abandoned by society due to being single mothers or divorced. Since then, the foundation has helped educate over a million women through grants and scholarships that lift them out of poverty…"

Do we talk like this? Not unless we want people to yawn and excuse themselves from the conversation.

To determine if dialogue is the best way to impart certain information, read it aloud and make sure it's entertaining, reflects the unique speech patterns of each character and sounds natural. If it doesn't, you can either re-work the dialogue to make it sound more natural, or you can take the information out of quotes and make it part of the narrative:

"It's lovely, isn't it," Judy said, eyes reflecting the candlelight.

Hannah smiled, knowing Judy wasn't referring to the charity dinner taking place around them, but rather what the Women's Foundation stands for: the legacy of hard-nosed, down-and-out women who simply had had enough. Hannah thought of them, those women who walked the New York City streets back in 1899, helping women up out of doorways and inviting them and their children to join a community. All of them housed in that first drafty, abandoned building and laughing as though living in the most elegant hotel even as they spread meals thinner than a first crust of ice.

Reactions

How a character reacts to other people and situations tells a lot about him. If he fades to the background when visiting his family for Thanksgiving, readers might assume he's feeling shy or withdrawn. If he responds that way every time he sees his family, readers will understand he's a peripheral, almost nonexistent member.

Readers can also learn a lot about a character by how others react to her. Picture two little girls dressed in pink tights, leotards and ballet shoes. Giggling and whispering as they stand in the studio, they suddenly snap to attention, faces serious, posture perfect.

The instructor walks in.

The girls' reaction clearly reflects the instructor's old school attitude of total discipline and zero tolerance.

Impact of Surrounding Social or Physical Environment

If a plant begins to wilt despite being watered and fertilized — there no apparent sign of bugs, fungus or other maladies — the culprit could be the environment itself. The air temperature is too hot, the sun too direct, the roots too cramped. Conversely, the perfect environment can make a modestly-successful plant grow luxurious.

Literary characters are similarly affected by their surroundings, and how they react under changing conditions can tell a lot about them. When stranded in a desert, does the character curl up and wait to die, or does he make decisions that increase his chances of survival? If nasty rumors ruin her socially, does she fall into a deep depression or hold her head high and ignore everyone?

Blind Spots

A blind spot is what we can't see about ourselves. Think of someone who believes he's generous with his time and money, yet calculates to the penny his portion of a bill when out lunching with friends. When someone points out the apparent hypocrisy, he's indignant, which points to the most embarrassing, tragic and funny part: while we can't see our blind spots, others often can.

Everybody, no matter how enlightened, has a blind spot. That's because we can't see our behavior in its entirety. If we could, we would no doubt observe obvious inconsistencies, such as the number of times we stated our belief in the Golden Rule and then treated others with prejudice and unkindness.

While blind spots can be obvious, they're often subtle, such as when a mother subconsciously steers one of her children toward more advantageous opportunities.

What makes blind spots so interesting and important is that they reveal a person's vulnerabilities. If a tougher-than-tough guy is blind to the absurdity of his ulta-warrior attitude, it could be because he can't acknowledge his extra sensitive interior. If a woman is always angry despite claims to the contrary, maybe it's because she doesn't know she's unhappy.

Before choosing a blind spot for your fictional character — or contemplating the blind spot of a nonfiction character — study the people around you. Look for inconsistencies between what they say and what they do. If they're aware of the discrepancy, then they're being hypocritical, which is a conscious decision to say one thing and do another. But if people are truly not aware of the inconsistency, you've just discovered their blind spot.

Always Show, Don't Tell?

You may have noticed that of the methods you can use to reveal your character slowly, all involve showing readers rather than telling them. Take Jason. Instead of saying, "Jason can't remember when he became an arsonist," we describe the way he looks at the trees growing drier by the day. We reveal his isolation through dialogue between two kids at school. We show how he reacts to the increasingly tense social environment around him as wildfires creep closer to town.

That said, it's time to present the other side. While a lot of writing books and articles go on about the evils of telling and how writers should never do it, many classic and bestselling books involve a lot of telling.

So rather than get frustrated and confused by the now famous and seemingly arbitrary advice of *show, don't tell*, employ a simple rule: If you can show, *do*. If you can't, *tell*.

Fiction Example:

A great demonstration of a character's blind spot takes place during a chilling scene in Lois Lowry's famous novel, *The Giver*.

The story revolves around a boy named Jonas who's taught to obey the rules in order to preserve the peace and happiness of his community in an altered, presumably futuristic world.

Yet his belief in the goodness of society shatters one day when he secretly follows his father to work and watches him carry out a job-related task. Having been taught this task is normal and necessary, the father is blind to the possibility that the deed may be wrong. Yet because Jonas is not fully inculcated in the rationalizations of his society, he's horrified by what he sees.

The father's blind spot reveals his vulnerability, that although an intelligent, caring man, he allows society to think for him. The blind spot also adds tension by increasing Jonas' suffering, thus propelling him toward desperate measures that speed the story toward its climax.

Nonfiction Example:

David Lipsky's *Absolutely American: Four Years at West Point* provides an excellent illustration of how environment can affect people. Following a group of cadets through their four years, Lipsky chronicles every tradition of West Point life, including R-Day when new cadets arrive. After saying goodbye to their parents, the cadets are whisked off by an institution with the know-how to tear down an individual and erect a new soldier, all within a day's time.

Needless to say, the West Point environment is a stark contrast to what the new cadets are accustomed to. Their civilian clothes are taken and their cash banked. They're ordered around, given clothes, checked by doctors, shorn of hair and taught the basics of how to stand, listen and salute. Then they have to report successfully, which means saluting and saying one sentence: their name and that they're reporting to the Cadet in the Red Sash for the first time. Yet the physical and social environment — the noise and complete shift in how they're treated — are so stressful they turn new cadets' brains into mush, despite the fact that most are former valedictorians, class presidents and sports stars. Through dialogue between experienced cadets and new arrivals, we see the newbies' distress as they mess up, one after another, some getting so jangled they forget their own names.

Character Study 11

Believe it or not, we've reached the last character study for Adrina, because with the completion of this segment, we'll have grown her to maturity.

We've got a lot to do before then, however, so let's get started.

In the last character study we left her riding in a small plane over the Australian outback. She's gazing out the window, looking at miles of landscape as barren as she feels. Suddenly the plane jolts. The two engines sputter and go silent, for a moment suspending all the passengers in an eerie, sunny quiet.

The nose of the plane dips and the aircraft begins to lose altitude as the two businessmen, the mother and the daughter begin a cacophony of prayers, yells, screams and curses. Whereas Adrina, eyes wide, keeps her mouth tight as she pulls her chin back, hunches her shoulders and grips the armrests. And we're there with her, inside her, as she holds her breath, the sound of all that's happening blocked somehow so that it feels as though she's viewing a silent movie. She watches the mother; the mouth stretched wide, the face red, an arm thrown across her 10-year-old daughter in an attempt to offer extra protection. Of the two businessmen, one is throwing up, his head turned sideways due to the downward force that presses their heads against their seats. Then they become rag dolls as the plane bumps along. Though the ground still looks too far away, the pilot has no choice. He lands, they bounce, one smack and the plane halts.

Dazed, the passengers crawl out to see the plane's nose smashed against a small outcropping of rock, the pilot dead. There's shock and blood, the two men and girl seriously injured. The sun goes down, the sun rises. A small, decrepit plane happens along, flown by a shirtless, bearded Aboriginal man.

Adrina shades her eyes as the rattling plane lifts back into the air, the two wounded businessmen and mother and daughter aboard. Then pop, the strange muting in her head and the fuzziness of her thoughts disappears, sound and clarity returning to full volume as she listens to the engine's drone die away. She slowly turns in a full circle and sees rock and scrub stretched to the horizon, her only solace a small mound of food and other equipment meant to keep her alive until help arrives.

After three days, however, she realizes no one is coming.

Having introduced Adrina and brought her to the main physical and psychological conflict of the story, we'll continue to reveal Adrina by all the means available to us; through action, narrative description, and in time, monologue.

We'll watch as she considers her remaining food, water and supplies. A doer, she draws both on her fieldwork experience and her greatest strength — her fierce determination to never again be left behind — in an effort to find water and eventually make it to civilization. She walks at night and stays out of the sun during the day. She watches for birds and any other animals, knowing they'll lead her to water if she can only follow their path. She scans for dry waterbeds and when she finds them, digs. More and more desperate for water, she comes upon a rancid, almost dry watering hole. Though dying to drink, she forces herself to dig some feet away until water bubbles up, knowing that although murky, the water is clean, soil an excellent filter against the bacteria and germs that plague stagnant watering holes.

Somewhere along the way, Adrina begins talking aloud to her mother; at first formally, distantly, as if meeting someone she only met once or twice a long time ago. Her stiff, respectful tone takes on a bitter note that bleeds into questions and philosophy, which finally crumbles into pitiful pleas for understanding. The more Adrina talks and the more actions she takes, the more we see the level of her pain and loss and what makes her admirable as hell. The more we root for her to survive as the days of water deprivation and heat rise along with the tension level, every step she takes bringing her nearer to what she fears most, that she deserves to be left behind. That she's dying amid nothingness because she is nothing.

Then one morning near dawn, she looks down and finds herself walking on a dirt road almost completely covered by sand. She stops and looks up. Though she sees nothing but more barren landscape, she knows where the road leads, both literally and proverbially. Survival.

And she glimpses, for the first time, why a mother might abandon her child to such a godforsaken life. Not because she wanted to, but because she had to. Not so she could survive, but so Adrina could. Not out of hatred, then, but out of love, the last act of a desperate mother trying to protect her daughter.

So that as Adrina stands on the border between death and survival, she understands that at some point, when you've gone far enough, you pass the halfway mark where you're no longer going away from, but rather going toward something, a departure becomes an arrival.

Adrina starts to hobble faster with whatever energy she has left. And we follow behind, clapping and rooting for her; urging her on. Whether she lives or dies now, at least she's beaten the fear that's kept her only half alive for so long. And before our very eyes, she unfurls into a hundred different shades of magnificent, her root system deep, her reach far.

Your Character

Exercise 11: Unfurling the Foliage

As with Adrina's character study, this exercise will be the last step in growing your character to maturity. You'll do so by allowing her to unfurl her foliage slowly over the course of the story, thus allowing readers to develop a deeper understanding of who she is and how she suffers.

Begin by opening the *Possible Scenes* worksheet you began in *Chapter 7*. Now that the scenes are in chronological order, their name, time, action and importance set, it's time to add what new information each scene reveals. For example:

Scene Name: Joanie meets Crackerjack

Action: Joanie meets Crackerjack, the lame horse owned by a neighbor. The horse bites Joanie when she tries to feed him an apple.

Importance: Readers meet Crackerjack, Joanie's antagonist. The horse bite enrages Joanie and spurs her deepest desire, to never let anyone or anything hurt her again. So motivated, Joanie sets out to make Crackerjack do her bidding.

New Information: the reason for Joanie's crazed motivation is that six years ago, when she was 13, a guy grabbed her mother's purse in a parking garage. Being strong-minded, Patty McNeil fought back. The thief shot her dead.

By working through each scene as such, you'll quickly discern any unwanted patterns. For example, by scanning all the scene names and action descriptions, you'll be able to determine whether you equally balance the story among the various characters and subplots, or whether you stick with one character/subplot for too long, which might cause readers to forget what's happening elsewhere in the story. Or you may get to the *importance* segment and realize there is no good reason for the scene or that it can be combined with another.

You can use the *new information* segment to make sure you're revealing all the necessary details about your character and doing so at an effective rate.

Revealing all the necessary details about your character: To make sure you're doing so, consult your *Other Significant Details About the Character* worksheet. As you place details in the story, make sure to check them off your list so you don't accidentally use them twice.

Revealing details at an effective rate: Read through your list of scenes to check how fast you're revealing information about your character. If you pack a lot of details into scenes one, two and three and very few in subsequent scenes, you've probably created an info dump and so need to spread out the information more. If you have very little character information in the first third of the story, you're probably not giving readers enough information to keep them interested.

Even though you'll tell more about the character in the first third of the story than in the latter two-thirds, every scene should reveal something new.

When convinced your scenes are complete, necessary and well paced, it's time to finally — *finally* — start writing if you haven't already. The planning over, it's imperative you follow your character from one action to the next in order to test his strength and durability.

Let the writing flow without any attempt to edit. Freed of self-criticism and guided by the scene descriptions, immerse yourself in the sights, sounds and smells of your story. Imagine the way she talks to people. Jump from the plane with him. Listen to her whistle the secret code. One by one slip in those details that make your character unique.

Considering how difficult it is to have your character realistically interact with as yet undeveloped characters, take time out to develop them using the same process we've employed thus far, which will get faster and easier every time you use it.

Then continue writing and watch as one paragraph turns into two; those two pages lengthening into three; that fourth chapter followed by a fifth, sixth and seventh.

As you write, you'll watch your character settle deep into her life where she'll grow even more now that all constraints are gone. Keep writing, monitoring her growth and developing other characters.

Although you may think that this is the last step — that when you're done writing, your character will be ready for public display — ask the question you've asked before, *What more can I possibly do to make my character the best he can be?*

Two last tasks should come to mind.

Chapter 12
Pruning

Gardeners know better than anyone that in order to make something the best it can be, it has to be pruned, which means cutting away both dead and living matter. While chopping off ugly, dried branches that pose a fire hazard makes sense, the trimming of living branches, leaves and flowers is less inviting precisely because they are alive. Why would we purposely kill something that's still growing?

The answer is, because doing so shapes the plant; maintains its health; improves the quality of its stems, foliage and flowers; and restricts detrimental growth.

Why It's Necessary

While plants in the wild are beautiful when grouped in a forest or field setting, they're often not much to look upon individually. Competing for scarce resources, they grow spindly, crooked, have gaps in their foliage, grow stunted in the shadow of other plants or even die.

We, on the other hand, are attempting to grow characters that are gorgeous when viewed alone. We've nurtured them thus far and so feel no need to withdraw our help now. That's why we'll make whatever cuts are necessary for our character's overall health and well-being, a process also known as editing. Our goal is to remove anything that's unnecessary, ineffective, or no longer useful to, nor healthy for, the character.

How NOT to Prune

As knowledgeable gardeners know, it's better not to prune than to do so incorrectly. Imagine handing an inexperienced adolescent a chain saw, instructing him to prune an overgrown bush then leaving him alone to do the job. While there's a miniscule chance he'll do okay, the odds are he'll hack away for the sheer joy of it. The result? Irreversible ruination of the plant's shape and health.

So instead of making huge slashes, a good pruning job involves small, carefully considered cuts. Why? Because small cuts mean small, fixable mistakes, whereas big cuts mean big, possibly permanent blunders.

If tempted to make big changes, consider what we've learned, that significantly altering a character, especially after she's fully matured, will damage what makes her consistent, believable and admirable, the qualities that make her great. Having spent so much time growing her with care, why would we haphazardly cut her down?

That in mind, if you find yourself in the position of either slashing the character to comply with a publisher's demands or getting published, don't be cowed. Stick up for your character! Explain how you grew her. Prove how every action leads to the climax. Argue for the details that make her lush and complex. If the publisher still demands the story be cut, consider looking for a new publisher. If you don't, you might get your work published, but it'll be a bitter win, because you'll know how fabulous your character was before you hacked her down.

How to Prune

We greatly reduce the need for significant pruning by planning well, which we've already done. Yet despite our efforts, we'll still have to do some amount of pruning. Most of the cuts will be obvious and easy to make, while some will be hard to identify and fix. Still others will be painful to even contemplate.

What will give us the strength to do what's necessary is the proper perspective, that pruning improves the health and welfare of the character. We can either wait to prune until after finishing the first draft of the story or by trimming as we go.

After the First Draft

As we write, we can let our character grow lush and wild by including as many details about him as possible. When done, however, we'll probably have a large pruning job on our hands. Rather than get overwhelmed, we'll be patient and begin by clearing away the small, obviously unnecessary material, then continue to make small cuts. Occasionally we'll step back to check the shape and health of the character by asking, *Does this detail/action stem from the defining detail and lead to the climax?*

Imagine we've written a story titled *The Fight*, which involves a Hispanic boy named Hector. A support character, his defining detail is a slightly teasing, in-the-know smile that's truly unusual. At the climax of the story, Hector and his best friend, Ramon (the protagonist), face an armed bully. Hector smiles, which throws the bully off balance long enough for Ramon to strike.

When done writing, we'll go over the story and tag any words/sentences/paragraphs for removal and insert the reason they should be cut. For example:

> Ramon kicks a stone as they walk. Frowning, he looks sideways at Hector. "You did not."
>
> "I did, too." Hector smiles, knowing Ramon will have to smile, too. Ramon doesn't know it, but Hector's smile is

magic. He inherited it from his *abuela*, who, on the day Hector was born, informed his mother that Hector possessed la *sonrisa mágica*. When old enough to understand, Abuela told him the news, too. She warned him of his responsibility to use the gift wisely, which meant smile often, never brag and never, never smile in the face of hatred. Just as solemnly, Hector accepted his duty.

The fifth of six children, Hector also proved magical with a bat. Though the one he owned was squashed at the tip, the result of his oldest brother using it to ram a hole in the ground while trying to make a hole for a fence post, Hector could nonetheless use the bat to place the ball wherever he wanted on the field. (CUT PARAGRAPH: breaks up action; baseball fact interesting, but it doesn't lead to the climax in any way.)

Hector kept smiling until the corner of Ramon's lips turned up, though suspicion lingered in his black eyes.

Once flagged, we can think about the proposed change and if necessary, do a self-conversation before making a final decision.

As You Go

If we don't want a huge pruning job, shape and trim the character as you write by employing the tools that help bypass the extraneous: the one-sentence test; a poignant defining detail; a clear motivation; and self-conversation. While writing the scene in which Hector walks down the road with his friend, we'll stop to consider the detail regarding his ability to bat. If it doesn't stem from his defining detail or lead to the climax, we'll pass it by and keep writing.

Save What You Cut

Rather than delete what you cut, open your project's file and create a new document titled *Cut Material*. Use this document as a place to store any phrase/sentence/paragraph you cut from the story, making sure to label the material so you'll remember where it came from. For example:

Chapter 1

— he said he wouldn't, that he couldn't.

— The fifth of six children, Hector also proved magical with a bat. Though the one he owned was squashed at the tip, the result of his oldest brother using it to ram a hole in the ground while trying to make a hole for a fence post, Hector could nonetheless use the bat to place the ball wherever he wanted on the field.

Chapter 2

— Ramon thought of his little brother, then of God, and how God could take the life of a 3-year-old boy with a dimple in each cheek.

— extra food, as if Ramon had ever heard of that

By holding on to what we cut, we can add it back later if necessary. If we decide to make Hector's baseball ability integral to the climax, for example, we can reinstate the related paragraph or move it to a more appropriate location where it doesn't slow down the action.

Saving what we cut also helps us cope better with pruning, which can be a psychologically rigorous task. After all, who looks forward to cutting what's taken time and effort to create? Faced with carting off perfectly good pieces, we'll often keep them, even if detrimental to our character. Whereas if we know the material is not gone forever, but merely set aside, we're much more likely to make necessary cuts.

Besides storing cut material in one document, we should also keep every revision of the story. Then if anything happens — we get lost, make a mistake that's too complex to fix, decide we like the original idea better — we can return to the earlier version and extract what we need. The process is as follows:

1. Write and save the story under an appropriate title (i.e., *The Fight*)

2. Duplicate the story and give it an appropriate title (i.e., *The Fight.2*)

3. Rewrite and edit the new version.

4. When finished, continue through as many versions — .3, .4, .5, etc.— as is necessary to tell your character's story the way you envision. Along the way, if you decide you like a scene as written in a previous version, copy that section to your newest revision.

If using a notebook, be sure to file cut material in a way that will help you find it quickly. If using a computer, it will automatically organize documents alphabetically and numerically, as such:

Chapter 1
Chapter 1.2
Chapter 1.3
Character Worksheet
Cut Material
The Fight
The Fight.2
The Fight.3

Disease: Problems That Can Plague Your Character

While developing a character requires us to pull close to him, pruning demands that we step back and take an overall look. When we do, we may find he's afflicted by one or more maladies. Think of gardeners, who, after studying a brown spot on a single leaf, stand back to find the entire branch so plagued. Though such a sight can induce panic, remember that locating the problem is the hard part. Then it's only a matter of finding and administering the right remedy.

A Sloppy Presentation

A sloppy presentation regarding spelling, grammar, punctuation and format is probably the most common disease to plague characters.

Considering how many books are devoted to this subject, we'll save space and time by boiling the lesson down to its essence: if you don't proofread and format your story properly, NOBODY will look at it. Nobody includes those you most want to read your work: agents, publishers and readers.

Imagine spending all this time nurturing and growing your character, then you can't find one person to look at her because the manuscript is in such bad shape. The cover sheet is stained with coffee. There's one spelling error after another. The text is single-spaced instead of double-spaced. The story is printed on both sides of a sheet instead of only one. There are no page numbers. There's Rampant Capitalization Of Everything.

Though tiny, these errors are thorns that stick people as they attempt to read your story. Unable to concentrate on your character, they'll stop reading.

Therefore, when you get the content of your story exactly as you want it, clean up the manuscript by going over it slowly and correcting any mechanical errors. The goal is to make your story effortless to read.

Proper spelling, punctuation and grammar: If agents and publishers see a manuscript filled with spelling errors, dropped periods, obviously unintended sentence fragments and other mechanical problems, they'll stop reading. After all, would you want to read something as arduous as, "And she roze from the sofa laufing to say she wnted to go home: while he told Her not too. He said his Organization would call her Department, myabe even her Supervisor, they could…" That and sloppiness identifies writers as newbies who are far from producing publishable material. If you argue spelling, grammar and punctuation are not your strong point, they'll say, *Too bad.*

If you truly have a difficult time with the mechanics of writing, you could hire a professional book editor after first asking for recommendations, checking references and negotiating payment and a deadline for completion. Though rates for such services vary enormously, don't automatically choose the lowest bid. You want an experienced professional who not only knows what agents and publishers are looking for, but has connections in the industry.

If you don't have that kind of money, find a dictionary and a concise punctuation and grammar reference. There are multitudes of both in hard copy form (i.e., Webster dictionary) and on the Internet (i.e., Webster.com), including Harvey Stanbrough's concise *Punctuation for Writers: A Thorough Primer for Writers of Fiction and Essays*, published by Central Avenue Press.

Whatever you do, don't rely only on word processing software equipped with spelling and grammar functions since they only find some errors. For example, most spell checks don't catch homonyms, such as, "Their hare turned green," when the author meant to say *hair.*

What's been said so far goes double for query letters, which are letters of introduction that ask agents or publishers to read your work. If your query is a disheveled mess, they'll assume the manuscript is, too. Whereas if you make your query as clean and professional as you would appear if showing up in person to introduce yourself, agents and publishers will be duly impressed.

Proper Formatting

Formatting refers to how the writing looks on a page. When writing a query letter, it should follow a standard business letter format in 12-point Courier font: the sender's address and the date in the upper right corner, the recipient's name and address below and to the left, a standard greeting of Dear _____, etc. (For an example of a query letter and its components, turn to Appendix A.)

Regarding most fiction and nonfiction manuscripts — essays, articles, short stories — agents and editors expect to see the following format:

Pat Drew   4,432 words
122 Skiddo Dr.
Anyhoo, LA
(333) 222-1111

How to Build a Fireplace From Scratch

I've found that the best way to build a fireplace from

scratch is to first determine what materials are most

prevalent in the area where you live....

Note the single-spaced author information, the lack of "©" to signify copyright and the double-spaced text, which makes the material easier to read and allows agents and editors room to make notes.

Now compare that to the formatting required for a screenplay:

1   INT. COFFEE SHOP   1

KATHY, age 22, pushes through the front door of the local diner set in a small Minnesota town. Wearing a raincoat, she's dripping from a spring downpour. She takes off her coat and hangs it on a coat rack as THREE HIGH SCHOOL GIRLS look at her and erupt in giggles.

KATHY
(nervously glances at girls)
Hiya, Mary.

MARY, the diner owner, a thin, full-blooded Hopi, stands at the stove with her back to the door. She turns to Kathy.

MARY
(not smiling)
I hear you got trouble.

Note the large margins, the single-spaced blocks of dialogue, the uppercase names upon first introduction, etc.

Needless to say, the formatting for one story can be quite different than for another. So after deciding what type of story you're going to write, find out the right way to format it. Make sure to research the correct way to format any supporting documents, too, such as the bibliography, appendix and glossary.

Again, there are hundreds of books and online sources that can tell you what to do. Consider that when I typed the phrase *proper manuscript format* into a computer search engine, I got over 600,000 listings. Perusing the first 10 resulted in eight web sites offering accurate — and free — information.

When it comes to screenplays, you can certainly format the document manually or use your word processor's styles function. But current screenplay-writing software, which automatically formats your work, makes the job a lot easier. If you plan to write more than one screenplay, think about making the investment.

Lastly, if you want to prove to an agent/publisher/editor that you're seeking her services for specific reasons, as opposed to making her feel like one recipient in a mass mailing, take time to format your query letter to her specifications. If you don't know what they are, consult a reference book that lists market information, such as *Writer's Market*. Better yet, go to the web site of her literary agency or publishing house and check the submission guidelines. Then do exactly what they say.

Too Much Repetition

Repetition is one of the most annoying diseases to plague characters. Imagine how much readers appreciate the first time we describe our heroine's most striking feature, her gorgeous, long, flowing red hair. They appreciate a second mention of the gorgeous, long, flowing red hair because it reminds them of what makes her stand out in a crowd, while the third explains why the handsome guy falls in love with her. No doubt there are still a number of legitimate reasons for mentioning her gorgeous, long, flowing red hair. Yet hopefully you're beginning to understand that if we mention her gorgeous, long, flowing red hair too often, her gorgeous, long, flowing red hair will begin to annoy readers. If it continues, her gorgeous, long, flowing red hair will become loathsome, then maddening, so that by the hundredth mention of those locks, readers will be ready to shave her bald.

The same can happen if we repeat our character's favorite sayings too often. After all, how many times can she say, "Oh'm'god," before readers throw up?

To see if repetition is a problem in your story, read it through. If any repetition feels excessive, it probably is. Shave here and there and re-read the story, continuing the process until reaching whatever number of repetitions feels necessary and reasonable.

Loss of Balance

Stepping back also allows you to see whether a character is properly balanced and if not, how he's become overgrown in some areas and scrawny in others. While fully developed as an action-oriented person, there may not be enough personal history to explain his actions. Or maybe her physical features are well described, but there are too few clues about what she's thinking.

Determining whether a character is balanced is a subjective task. Therefore, the best approach is to read your story and record your impressions. If you decide there's too much of one thing and not enough of another, take time to cut, add and rearrange material.

When done, step back again to see if your character is balanced among other characters. Specifically, does he fulfill his job description? Take a support character like Hector. Does he support the protagonist, or outshine him? If the latter, either decrease Hector's prominence or increase that of the protagonist.

That said, sometimes characters exceed our expectations and grow to a size and complexity we could never have predicted. This is a particularly common occurrence when writing nonfiction. While researching and writing about one character, we'll come across another that commands our attention. Think of moderately important support characters or small side characters who prove so interesting and aggressive they simply take over the story. Or they begin as antagonists, and as we get to know and empathize with them, become protagonists. While strong enough to assert their uniqueness, what should we do with them?

We could: allow them to change the focus of our story; prune them so they remain within their job description; or take them out of the story. If choosing either of the last two options, remember that we can always tell their story at a later date.

Whatever we choose, we should keep our main objective in mind, to tell one main story. Attempting to tell more than one by allowing characters to grow beyond their functions will confuse readers and deplete the power of our protagonist's story.

Weeds: Growth That Strangles Characters

Believe it or not, there are no plants officially labeled as weeds. Rather, weeds are simply those plants we don't want around, whether dandelions, tomatoes or even roses.

Like their organic counterparts, literary weeds are undesirable, often considered unattractive and always annoying. Not only do they grow where they shouldn't, but they can surround and choke a character. Specifically, a weed is anything that diverts nutrients away from the climax, thus weakening the story. Consider the following.

Getting sidetracked: Imagine Ramon is on his way to meet the bully and Hector is running to catch up. Yet as Hector runs, we allow him to remember something interesting, but only slightly necessary to the climax of the story. The diversion away from the main character dilutes the action and tension, drawing power away from the climax.

Too many subplots: Too many subplots can also draw attention away from the main plot. If the story is about Ramon overcoming his fear of adulthood by plunging into it and surviving, we should keep to those subplots that lead to the climax. If we instead attempt to follow a slew of other subplots — about the storekeeper's financial woes, the stray dog that's dying — we risk overshadowing Ramon's journey. Generally, the shorter the story, or the more complex the main plot, the fewer the subplots we should use.

Too many characters: Excess characters divert attention away from the main players. Usually the problem arises when authors include too many support and side characters. To steer clear of this problem, we should ask the following questions:

— Do we mention more than seven characters at the beginning of our story? If so, consider holding off on some of their introductions so readers won't be overwhelmed.

— Could several characters be combined? If it's difficult to keep track of our protagonist's seven siblings, maybe we could cut the family down to a sister and brother.

— Is it necessary to give the character a name? Doing so means readers will expect the character to have an integral function. If she doesn't, cut the name, so that Judy the librarian becomes simply the librarian.

— Do we often describe peripheral characters in too much detail rather than just enough to set the scene? If one sentence can do the job of a whole paragraph, let it.

Wordiness: Wordiness means using more words than are necessary to say something. For example, "The boy, always in a hurry, quickly strode from one end of the block to another," as compared to, "The boy hurried down the block."

Wordiness is acceptable if it's a signature of the character's speech, the style in which the story is told or not too annoying. If none of those apply, you've probably fallen prey to wordiness.

To correct the problem, ponder whether there's an easier way to say something while asking yourself:

Do I use too many adjectives and adverbs? (i.e., an elegant clock, a blue ocean, he shouts angrily, she laughs merrily)

Do I routinely go into too much unnecessary detail? (i.e., "She hands the woman Earl Grey tea in a blue and white bone china teacup of oriental motif along with an oblong almond biscuit slightly flavored with anise.")

If you answer yes to one or both questions, the following exercise will help you break the wordiness habit by teaching you how to separate the necessary from the unnecessary: Choose twenty long sentences from your writing and cut each down to as few words as possible. If the sentence still sounds fine, make the cut permanent.

The best way to whack wordiness, however, is by reading your work aloud. If you trip over words, get confused or start getting bored, you've hit a weed patch.

Cliché

Cliché is the trickiest disease to diagnose because it's so insidious. It slips into our subconscious through conversations and popular media and slips out again when we write. It's often so omnipresent that we don't even recognize it, so that when we write, "She had long, raven hair and cherry lips," we think we're geniuses when really such descriptive phrases have been used beyond excess.

We also tend to emphasize cliché qualities, like the blond hair and blue eyes of the beach babe or the tight bun and scowl of the school librarian.

While some clichés, as well as other problems discussed in this chapter, become apparent as soon as we step back, what do we do about those we can't see? We ask others for help.

Chapter 13
Preview Your Character

Wouldn't it be great if a buzzer went off at the precise moment our characters became great?

Unfortunately, that'll never happen, which means we need other people to look over our character for errors we missed and problems we simply can't see due to our own blind spots, biases and ignorance. Specifically, we want these reviewers to tell us what they like about our character, what could make her better and what they see about her that we don't.

Opening the Character to Critique

Opening our character to critique is tough because after putting in so much effort, it can be disappointing to learn he still needs more work. To dim the psychological distress, take to heart the old adage of *it's better to find out sooner that later*. After all, which would you prefer, to have your story repeatedly rejected by agents only to go back over your work and realize what needs to be changed? Or is it better to gather suggestions, make hard decisions and keep working until the people who critique your work agree it's an excellent story that will snag the interest of agents and publishers?

Now understanding the necessity of having your work critiqued, you need to find the right people for the job. You can, as previously suggested, hire a professional freelance editor. Yet that can be expensive, especially if your story is long or you've got a lot of projects to be critiqued. If so, ask for help from those around you.

Choose People You Trust

While it seems natural to ask our parents, spouse, significant other, children or other loved ones to read our work and offer suggestions, they often don't want to risk hurting our feelings and so won't tell the whole truth.

That's why we should choose people who we're not emotionally involved with. They can be avid readers, experts in the subject we're writing about, fellow writers and writing instructors. We can even form or join critique groups in which members take turns critiquing each other's work. These groups can meet in person or take place online or through email.

Whoever we choose, they should be people we trust to tell us not only what's good about our character, but also what needs work.

Those who critique should also have an appreciation for the type of story we're writing. If it's a literary short story that illuminates a character's personal change through internal actions, we should look for people who read such literature because they can compare ours to others in the same category and so make appropriate suggestions. Whereas if we choose people primarily interested in action-packed thrillers, they may compare our story to that genre and so make inappropriate suggestions, i.e., we need less character description and more car chases. If we try to explain our goal, they may think we don't know what's best and so continue pushing their suggestions until everyone winds up frustrated.

Lastly, choose people who can not only point out specific problems, but also offer solutions in a way we can understand and accept. Say they believe we tell readers too much about what she's thinking, which slows the action. Then they suggest we take out half of her internal thoughts and use more details that show us what she's thinking, so that instead of writing, "She doesn't know what to think of him, other than that he makes her nervous," she could instead "glance at him as she twists her hair into a tight coil."

This is an example of a positive comment and suggestion. A positive comment should not be confused with a compliment or flowery euphemism that skirts a tough criticism, as when a reader says, "She's really interesting," when actually the reader found her inconsistent.

Instead, a positive comment offers hope and stems from the assumption that with work, your character will be terrific, whereas a negative comment implies there's no hope. For example:

Positive comments:

— The protagonist isn't strong enough to carry the story yet.

— The character needs to double the number of actions he takes in order to seem like a doer instead of a whiner.

— I worry about your character's underlying motivation. You say she's motivated to tell the truth, no matter what, yet nothing big happens to test that motivation. What action could you use to really test her resolve? Maybe you could have her subpoenaed to testify against her ex-husband, which would really tempt her to lie.

Being told your protagonist isn't weighty enough to carry the story cannot be construed as too easy or not telling it like it is. Rather, the suggestion is a whopper that will entail a lot of work to correct. Yet there's no question the comment implies that if you make the necessary changes, the character will be successful.

Negative comments:

— Your protagonist sucks.

— She's not only stupid, she's a whiner. Just kill her off.

— There doesn't seem to be any interesting idea behind the story. She says she doesn't want to lie, she doesn't, the end. I'd never willingly read a story like this. Nobody wants to read about housewives.

Even if well intended, comments such as "sucks," "stupid" and "I'd never willingly read a story like this" do no good and all harm by leading us to believe our character and story are too far gone to save.

Then again, maybe those who make such comments believe they're doing us a favor by telling it like it is. If we haven't given them any input about how to critique, how can we complain?

Which begs the question, why haven't we told them what we want?

Setting the Rules

Imagine handing our neighbors sharp clippers and telling them to trim whatever they think necessary to make our prized Japanese maple better. They'll probably do a lousy job because their tastes are different than ours, they have no pruning experience or, having no stake in the tree's final outcome, they feel free to slash with abandon.

The point is that people who critique our character will assume they have carte blanche unless we tell them otherwise. In order to help them — as well as ourselves — we should stipulate how we want them to critique and what we want from the critique.

How to Critique

When preparing people to critique our work, we should explain what constitutes a positive, helpful suggestion. We can also request that when they note a problem, they offer a suggestion of how to fix it. We can then negotiate a deadline for completion and delivery of their comments, whether verbally, via a one-page letter summarizing their overall impression or as notes written on the manuscript.

As a courtesy, and to make sure you get the most from each critique, give your volunteers a manuscript free of mechanical errors so they can concentrate on the story. The *how* of the critique taken care of, we can then tell people what we *want* from the critique.

The Outcome

What we want from a critique will depend on where we are in the writing process. If we've just finished the first draft of our story, we may want people's general impressions of our character knowing there's still a lot of work to be done. If our character has undergone numerous critiques, we may be ready to submit the manuscript and so ask people to look for any small errors that may have slipped through. Some of our requests will be granted and others won't. While people usually do their best, they may fall into abusive language, be too vague about problem areas or procrastinate. If so, go over the rules again and provide clarification where necessary. If our readers still don't follow our guidelines, thank them for their time and effort and move on, knowing that some work relationships are simply not compatible.

Prepare a List of Questions

If volunteer reviewers don't know much about writing or critiquing, help them out by preparing a one- or two-page list of questions. Ask readers to peruse the list so they'll know what to focus on when reading. When they finish the manuscript, have them answer the questions.

Here are a few examples (for a full list, turn to Appendix B):

1. In one sentence, what's this story about?

2. Do you admire the character? Why or why not?

3. Can you identify with the character? If so, in what way?

4. What's the character trying to do?

Before people hand in their responses, you should answer the questions, too. While ideally their answers will match yours, be prepared for some disparity. If there's a good deal of disparity, the character still needs significant work. The good news is that our readers' answers point out where the character needs help and how to fix it.

Prune Again

You can arrange to have one person critique each revision, or have several people critique the story simultaneously. If they're willing, have volunteers read several revisions, a task critique groups members are often willing to perform.

When responses start rolling in, don't assume they're correct and automatically act upon the suggestions. Incorporating bad suggestions along with the good in an attempt to make everybody happy — known as writing by committee — can make your great character bland and unfocused. Instead, remember that as your character's primary caretaker, your job is to guide the pruning process by determining which suggestions are valid.

Toward that end, read people's comments and allow yourself time to absorb the feedback as well as how you feel about it. While it would be great if your character comes off exactly as you intended, the odds are you'll feel overwhelmed and depressed by how much work you still have to do, which I call *The Day After a Critique Hangover.* If so suffering, take a day off to recuperate. Get a massage. Play a round of golf. Indulge in an uninterrupted hour of reading your favorite book in your favorite chair while eating your favorite snack. Then when you're feeling better, make a list of people's suggestions and get to work. Or better yet, insert their comments directly into the manuscript as such:

> Leroy slouched across the street, a heavy frown on his face, hands stuffed in the pockets of his brown faux leather coat, his high-heeled platform shoes producing a heavy thud with every step, his black bell bottoms sweeping the broken glass-strewn concrete (3 of 4 people said there are too many descriptive phrases here and elsewhere. They suggested breaking such sentences into several or getting rid of some of the description).

If most readers make the same comment, it signals a definite problem that needs to be addressed, either by adopting their suggestion or devising your own solution. If only one or two comment about something, you can reread the passage and see if it strikes you as such.

Even if you don't agree, take time to understand readers' opinions, lest you dismiss problems that turn out to be significant. That and you want to make sure readers' concerns get addressed at some point. If they say the beginning is too confusing, but you don't want to give away the surprise too soon, you can take steps to lessen their confusion and shorten the time they have to wait for an explanation.

As you revise, have faith that your character is well rooted and can withstand the changes you're implementing.

You'll Know You're Done When...

When done with the first round of critique and rewrite, open your character to a second round and repeat the process as often as is necessary. You'll know your character is ready to meet the public when most of those who critique your work — because it will never be all — appreciate your character as you do.

Keep in mind that no one person — whether a famous author, distinguished professor of literature or popular workshop facilitator — knows everything about developing great characters. Rather, everyone knows something, so feel free to pick and choose what works best for you.

Remember, too, that there's no such thing as perfection. You can only ever work to the fullest of your ability at any given time. So rather than cringe while rereading older material, appreciate how much you've grown since then. And instead of wishing you could write at a level you haven't reached yet, take pride in your determination to do better. Just as plants continue to grow throughout their lives, so we'll continue to grow in our ability to create great characters as long as we're willing to get our hands dirty and work hard.

Toward that end, continue to read, learn, observe and write, write, write, knowing the more you experiment with different seed combinations and growing techniques, the greater your success in growing gorgeous, one-of-a-kind characters.

Conclusion

Since beginning this book, you've learned a multitude of concrete skills regarding how to create and grow great characters. You began the groundwork by understanding what type of characters there are and what roles they play. Then you learned to look around for ideas about what could make your character unique. While compiling a list of details, you considered your options based on what the character needs to accomplish in the story.

Then you chose the precise detail that best defines your character. Seed in hand, you planted it and watched your character sprout a healthy, significant motivation leading to actions that make her admirable, identify her greatest strength and weakness and highlight her exceptional quality. The more actions she takes, the closer she gets to her greatest fear, which she tries to dodge, ignore, outwit and outrun before taking a stand to destroy it.

All this because you allow the character to move freely based on her nature rather than your desires. When necessary, you offer her your own personal experience or research necessary information to make scenes authentic. You know the best way to introduce her and over the course of the story reveal everything that makes her unique.

But you won't stop there. When finished writing, you'll prune your character to improve her overall health and well-being, even if it means trimming perfectly good writing, cutting out obvious disease and asking others to critique your work.

And hopefully somewhere along the way, you'll realize how much you've grown. Instead of getting lost in that mysterious artistic process, you now have the specific skills and tools necessary for developing future characters, not to mention the know-how to persevere in an often harsh and volatile industry in which it's imperative you stick by your characters.

For proof, consider how much we've grown through the development of Adrina. She began as a nameless protagonist and became an emotionally shutdown child-woman who masquerades as a professional while attempting to outrun her fear of abandonment. Finally lost, she walks through the barren sand of a foreign land until coming upon a lonely, dusty road.

As Adrina squints into the distance, she realizes the road can take her away from or lead her toward something. Maybe that's what her mother saw, too. And Adrina thinks about an isolated Vietnamese woman married to an emotionally dead man who complained of her dark spells, her inability to act like a wife and mother, always mumbling, never working. Could she have been mentally ill? Yes. Could she have been suicidal? Yes. Could she have felt she might harm her small daughter? Yes.

So that as Adrina stares down the road, the feeling takes hold, of a woman who flees in order to protect her small daughter. Not out of hate, then, but out of love. And Adrina begins to walk, then walk faster, knowing the only way to find out is to make it out, make it back, to ask and inquire about what happened to the woman who screeched out of sight. And we know Adrina will make it out, every molecule of her being motivated to cancel her fear of abandonment once and for all. That and she feels a growing obligation to save her own life so she can meet the person who saved her life the first time, a woman as abandoned in a barren foreign land as Adrina is now.

Through Adrina, as well as the lessons, examples and exercises in each chapter, we learned the most important concept contained in this book, that great characters cannot be created from inanimate matter. They can't be manufactured like a new car or put together like a craft project. Rather, they're born from want, need and opportunity and once given life, grip us tighter and closer than we ever thought possible.

Great characters owe us nothing, yet bestow a tremendous insight and emotional involvement. We see reflections of ourselves in them, yet they're not created in our image. They reach the point where we can't change them, yet are versatile enough to take whatever we throw at them. They deserve our admiration and deep respect, even when they're despicable.

Great characters are more than living beings. They're the promise of life. As such, they'll always rise to the occasion so long as we allow the leaves and limbs of our personal history to intermingle with theirs, which means understanding the superiority of Mother Nature over human achievement.

To do so, envision yourself as a gardener standing on a hill. Rather than be a master of nature, you're a part of it, like the grass beneath your feet, the birds flying overhead and the sun shining down. As you watch, a seed floats your way. Containing pure potential, it's encased in soft white fuzz that allows it to drift on the breeze. Driven by curiosity, you reach out and catch the seed. From that moment on, it's up to you whether and how well the plant will grow. The more ardent your attentions, the more passionate the results.

So that in the end, you'll gaze upon a being of immense complexity and unending possibilities, knowing you can't claim total credit for this magnificent life. Instead, you'll understand the relationship between the creator and the created, that one is nothing without the other. That your character — as well as your own growth — began the moment she drifted by and you reached out your hand.

Contact Information

I could hardly advocate that you seek suggestions, questions and clarifications about your work from others if I didn't myself. Therefore, if you have such comments, email me at Martha@Engber.com. I would particularly relish feedback about how this book has helped you and in what way.

Whenever you achieve success with your characters, let me know! I'm happy to congratulate you, and if you're willing, list your achievement on my web site, GrowingGreatCharacters.com.

About the Author

A journalist by training, Martha Engber had a play produced in Hollywood and a short story nominated for a Pushcart Prize. Her short stories have appeared in numerous literary journals such as *Watchword*, the *Berkeley Fiction Review*, *Anthology*, *Bookpress* and *Frontiers: A Journal of Women Studies*. Based in the San Francisco Bay area, she teaches writing workshops on a variety of topics, which include, among others, character development, copyediting, business writing and how to incubate great ideas. For a full list of workshops and credentials, visit her web site, GrowingGreatCharacters.com.

Acknowledgements

I would like to thank the following authors and publishers for permission to use quotes from the following sources:

Your Organic Garden With Jeff Cox, by the editors of Rodale Garden Books, Rodale Press, Emmaus, PA. Copyright © 1994.

Cottage for Sale: A Woman Moves a House to Make a Home, Kate Whouley, Commonwealth Editions, Beverly, MA. Copyright © 2004.

The Stranger Beside Me, Ann Rule, New American Library, New York. Copyright © 1989.

The English Patient, Michael Ondaatje, Knopf, New York, NY. Copyright © 1992.

The Girl Next Door, from *Dress Your Family in Corduroy and Denim*, David Sedaris, Little Brown & Co., Boston, MA. Copyright © 2004.

The Shipping News, E. Annie Proulx, Scribner, New York, NY; Maxwell Macmillan Canada, Toronto; Maxwell Macmillan International, New York, NY. Copyright © 1993.

Corn-pone Opinions, from *Europe and Elsewhere*, Mark Twain, Harper & Brothers, New York. Copyright © 1923.

Gardener to Gardener Seed-Starting Primer and Almanac, edited by Vicki Mattern, Rodale Press, Emmaus, PA. Copyright © 2002.

"She calls up... to the loft that night..." Reprinted with permission of Scribner, an imprint of Simon & Schuster Adult Publishing Group from *Angela's Ashes* by Frank McCourt. Copyright © 1996 by Frank McCourt.

Glossary

Antagonist: a character who tests and challenges the protagonist; acts as a roadblock on the protagonist's journey, thus causing tension that forces the protagonist to make choices and ultimately, change.

Backstory: what happens to a character before the story begins; a character's previous history and experience.

Belief system: the few underlying rules by which a character lives.

Blind spot: what a character can't see about himself.

Broken timeline: when a story is told nonsequentially; when scenes are arranged out of order in terms of time (i.e., scenes near the end of the story are placed near the beginning).

Catalyst: a character who precipitates change; adds tension by escalating change either in the character and/or the plot.

Character: (general) a living person; (as pertains to fiction) a living person born of imagination; (as pertains to nonfiction) a person born in real life and filtered through imagination.

Cliché: an overused idea or expression; a character whose behavior is predictable.

Climax: moment of character's most significant personal change.

Colloquialism: a saying or expression that mimics informal speech and reflects the surrounding culture.

Courtesy call: when authors let interviewees know when the story will be published; a professional "heads up."

Editing: the process of trimming excess detail and action to improve the overall health and well-being of a character.

Extrapolation: to infer from what's already been observed; using what's known about a character to determine what he'll do in the future.

First-person point of view: the character tells the story through his or her eyes, as in, "I then saw…"

Great character: a person remarkable for being consistent, admirable, believable.

Info dump: overwhelming readers by dumping too much information on them when first introduced to a character or situation.

Law of literary motion: the size of a character's change will cause an equal and opposite change in others.

Momentum: the impact of a character's action or change, which is determined by the size and intensity of the action or change.

Motivation: what moves a character to act; results in change.

Point of view: who tells the story.

Protagonist: a main character around which the story revolves; takes readers on a journey in which the character undergoes and completes a personal transformation.

Psychogenesis: the psychological origin of why a person thinks or behaves as she does; the foundation of a character's defining detail.

Scene: what happens in a particular moment in a particular place and time; a physical setting; the continuous actions that constitute a specific moment.

Scene sequence: the order of a story's scenes; they should be organic and lead naturally from one to the other, whether the story is told chronologically or via a broken timeline.

Side character: a peripheral character; sets tone of scene; populates locales; adds color; increases tension.

Support Character: a character who supports the protagonist, either wittingly or unwittingly; helps the protagonist complete her journey.

Third-person limited point of view: an unnamed narrator tells the story by following only one character and explaining what that character thinks and feels, as in, "Tom looked down, unable to endure her stare..."

Third-person objective point of view: an unnamed narrator tells the story by reporting on what's seen and heard, rather than what's felt, such as, "After looking at one another for a long moment, Harold gestured for Joan to sit."

Third-person omniscient point of view: the author tells the story by moving from one character to the next with the ability to explain what the characters are thinking and feeling, such as, "Lisa didn't want to say anything, nor did Steve, and George would go along with them."

Third-person point of view: an unnamed narrator tells the story.

Story List

Characters from the following stories were sited for examples throughout this book:

Fiction
The Adventures of Huckleberry Finn by Mark Twain
The Adventures of Tom Sawyer by Mark Twain
The Ax by Donald E. Westlake
The Ballad of the Sad Café by Carson McCullers
The Caine Mutiny by Herman Wouk
The Chosen by Chaim Potok
Christine by Stephen King
A Christmas Carol by Charles Dickens
The Color Purple by Alice Walker
The Curious Incident of the Dog in the Night-Time by Mark Haddon
Cyrano de Bergerac by Edmond Rostand
Don Quixote de la Mancha by Miguel de Cervantes Saavedra
Ender's Game by Orson Scott Card
The English Patient by Michael Ondaatje
Fight Club by Chuck Palahniuk
The Giver by Lois Lowry
The Glass Menagerie by Tennessee Williams
Gone With the Wind by Margaret Mitchell
Jack and the Fire Dragon by Gail E. Haley
Jane Eyre by Charlotte Bronte
The Joy Luck Club by Amy Tan
King Kong by Merian C. Cooper and Edgar Wallace
Little House on the Prairie by Laura Ingalls Wilder
Lord of the Flies by William Golding
Master and Commander by Patrick O'Brian
Moby Dick by Herman Melville
One Hundred and One Dalmatians by Dodie Smith
Pippi Longstocking by Astrid Lindgren

Plainsong by Kent Haruf
Rebecca by Daphne du Maurier
The Red Tent by Anita Diamant
Romeo and Juliet by William Shakespeare
The Secret Garden by Frances Hodgson Burnett
A Series of Unfortunate Events books by Lemony Snicket (Daniel Handler)
The Shipping News by E. Annie Proulx
Stargirl by Jerry Spinelli

Nonfiction
Absolutely American: Four Years at West Point by David Lipsky
Alive: The Story of the Andes Survivors by Piers Paul Read
All Brave Sailors: The Sinking of the Anglo-Saxon, August 21, 1940 by J. Revell Carr
All the President's Men by Bob Woodward and Carl Bernstein
Angela's Ashes by Frank McCourt
Billy the Kid: A Short and Violent Life by Robert M. Utley
Black Like Me by John Howard Griffin
A Child Called 'It': One Child's Courage to Survive by Dave Pelzer
The Conquest of Everest by Sir John Hunt
Corn-pone Opinions by Mark Twain
Cottage For Sale: A Woman Moves a House to Make a Home by Kate Whouley
Disturbed Ground by Carla Norton
The Explosive Child: A New Approach for Understanding and Parenting Easily Frustrated, Chronically Inflexible Children by Ross W. Greene
The Girl Next Door from *Dress Your Family in Corduroy and Denim* by David Sedaris
Gypsy: A Memoir by Gypsy Rose Lee
I Am the Central Park Jogger: A Story of Hope and Possibility by Trisha Meili
In Cold Blood by Truman Capote
The Liars' Club by Mary Karr
My Son, Yo-Yo by Marina Ma and Dr. John A. Rallo
Obsessive Genius: The Inner World of Marie Curie by Barbara Goldsmith
The Perfect Storm: A True Story of Men Against the Sea by Sebastian Junger

Roots by Alex Haley
The Secret Life of the Lonely Doll: The Search for Dare Wright by Jean Nathan
Starting Right With Turkeys by G. T. Klein
The Stranger Beside Me by Ann Rule
Swimming to Antarctica: Tales of a Long-Distance Swimmer by Lynne Cox
Sybil by Flora Rheta Schreiber
Truth and Beauty by Ann Patchett
A Walk in the Woods by Bill Bryson
Wheelchair Around the World by Patrick and Ann Simpson

Appendix A
Sample Query Letter: Components and Format

(Your name, address, date)
62 Pickle Dr.
Laredo, TX 00000
Sept. 15, 20-

(Recipient's name, address)
Frank Garcia
Frank Garcia Literary Agency
77 Super Star Lane
Los Angeles, CA 00000

(Greeting)
Dear Mr. Garcia,

(Introduction of who you are and what you want)
I'd like to request that you represent "The Fight," my literary novel about two boys and a magic smile.

(Immediate and catchy summary of your work)
Ramon and Hector, two 11-year-old boys from a tiny Texas town on the Mexican border, vow to remain best friends until death, neither thinking the end will come so soon. Ramon suffers the fear of a boy intimately familiar with deep physical and psychological pain, while Hector fears nothing due to his *sonrisa mágica*, which his abuela claims has been passed down in his family for generations. Capturing the atmosphere of dusty, unpaved streets, a hot wind and a smattering of cool, dark adobes, the novel, of approximately 88,000 words, has the forbidding feel of a Wild West showdown. When the banditos come to town, however, the good guys are but two unarmed boys.

(Why you're contacting the recipient in particular)

I believe you're ideally suited to represent "The Fight," given your experience in selling debut literary novels by Latino authors, such as, "Casa Bonita" by Jose Villarreal. Besides that author, I'm familiar with the work of your other clients, including Lucy Garcia and ChiChi Silva.

(Professional credentials)

Besides growing up the daughter of Mexican immigrants in a small Texas border town, I received a Master of Fine Arts degree from the University of Texas at Austin. I've had short stories published in *Prairie Schooner, Zyzzyva, Ploughshares* and other literary journals. I've had numerous nonfiction articles regarding Latino issues and culture published in Latino publications such as Diario La Estrella and Tiempos del Mundo.

(Specific request; sincere thank you)

As per the instructions on your web site, I've enclosed the first three chapters of "The Fight" and would like to request that I send the remaining manuscript. I've also enclosed a SASE **(self-addressed stamped envelope)**. If you have any questions, please let me know. Thank you for your time and consideration. I look forward to hearing from you.

Sincerely,

(Name, phone number, email/web address)

Alita Mendoza

(060) 112-2111

alita2b@skipjack.com

AlitaWrites.com

(P.S. Remember that query letters should be no more than one page in length and should include any specific information agents and publishers request via their web sites or reference guides.)

Appendix B
Sample List of Critique Questions

Dear Reader,

Please look over the following questions before you begin the manuscript to get an idea of what to focus on while reading. Then when you've finished the story, please answer the questions in one or more sentences either on this sheet or in a separate document. Please be as specific as possible.

Thank you in advance for your time and energy!

1. In one sentence, what is the story about?
2. Who is the protagonist (main character)?
3. What does he have to do over the course of the story?
4. What seems to define him as a person?
5. Do his internal beliefs seem to match his external actions? Why or why not?
6. Does he possess the knowledge he should regarding his work, locale, hobbies, etc.?
7. Do you admire him? Why or why not?
8. Does he possess any exceptional gifts or qualities?
9. What motivates him to act as he does?
10. Do his actions follow a logical path?
11. What does he most fear?
12. Does he experience a profound personal change? If so, when does it occur and what's the nature of the change?
13. What is most interesting about him?
14. What is least interesting about him?
15. Can you identify with him? If so, how?
16. Overall, what do you think of him?
17. What are your suggestions for improving him?
18. Of all the characters, which did you like best and why?
19. What are your suggestions for improving the other characters?

20. What's the main plot of the story, or sequence of actions that lead to the climax?
21. What other side stories take place?
22. What is most interesting about the story?
23. What is least interesting about the story?
24. What are your suggestions for improving the main plot?
25. Overall, what do you think of the story? Specifically, did you:
- enjoy reading it?
- learn anything new?
- want something more and if so, what?
26. As a reader, did anything frustrate you regarding:
- the characters
- the plot
- the format
27. If giving a letter grade from A (excellent) to F (failing), how would you rate the presentation of the manuscript regarding:
- spelling
- punctuation
- grammar
- format
28. Who do you think this story will appeal to?

(P.S. While readers will write down what they can, it's often only a fraction of what they think. Therefore, in order to extract even more information, as well as offer them a chance to clarify their responses, treat them to lunch, dinner, coffee, smoothies, whatever. If they live too far away, give them a call. Either way, readers are usually happy to talk about what they've read. And as they do, you can jot down a multitude of invaluable notes and ideas for improving your characters and story.)